Radio Drama

D1321494

Ian Rodger

M

First published 1982 by
THE MACMILLAN PRESS LTD
London and Basingstoke
Companies and representatives throughout the world

ISBN 0 333 29428 9 (hc)
ISBN 0 333 29429 7 (pbk)

Printed in Great Britain by Unwin Brothers Limited,
The Gresham Press, Old Woking, Surrey.

Contents

List of Plates

Acknowledgements

Plates 1, 2(b), 3, 5, 6(a), 6(b), 7(a) and 7(b) are reproduced by permission of the BBC Photographic Library. Plates 2(a) and 4 are reproduced by permission of the BBC Hulton Picture Library.

Every attempt has been made to trace copyright holders. The publishers would be willing to make the necessary arrangements in cases where it has not been possible to make an acknowledgement.

Preface

I was one of radio's children. Before I could read, my grand-mother clapped some headphones to my ears so that I could hear, amidst the crackling atmospherics, the magic of a distant voice speaking to me. Later, when I was of school age, the BBC's *Children's Hour* became an imperative daily ritual, bringing to me among other things the plays of L. du Garde Peach who made the past history of my country alive and immediate. When I had measles, my father carried the imitation-mahogany radio set into my bedroom so that I could hear the marvel of D. G. Bridson's *Coronation Scot.* The radio set had knobs by this time and I used to twiddle them to catch Radio Luxembourg and all the languages of Europe. When I was eleven, I tuned in accidentally to a speech by Hitler and, though I could not understand German, the voice conveyed to me a message of terror which my elders, who were mostly newspaper readers and not radio fanatics, found hard to appreciate. When the war came, I tuned into Warsaw and knew when the station went off the air that Poland had fallen. In Sussex during the Battle of Britain, I listened on a short wave receiver to a German pilot crying out '*Achtung,* Spitfire!' as he flew only a few thousand feet above me. Such moments brought home radio's immediacy but it was the journeys of the imagination encouraged by the works of people like Francis Dillon, Douglas Cleverdon and Louis MacNeice which shaped and directed my adolescent mind during the war.

Like many writers of my generation it was inevitable that I should choose radio as one of my means of communication. I gave my first radio talk for the English service of Sveriges Radio and my first radio play was produced in Dutch by AVRO, Hilversum. I am grateful to Sweden and Holland for giving me my first chance of a radio audience but I am naturally more indebted to the British producers who later took my work in hand and began to teach me the crafts of radio. I am grateful in particular to David Thomson, Francis Dillon, John Gibson, Terence Tiller, Robin Midgley, John Tydeman, Richard Imison, Alfred Bradley, Tony Cliff and Robert Cooper. I also had the luck to be the radio drama critic of the *Listener* during a time when something of a dramatic renaissance occurred in Britain. In the course of researching material for this book I am grateful for the help and assistance given to me by the BBC Written Archives Centre. I would also like to thank Michael Bakewell, Eric Ewens, Rene Cutforth, Douglas Cleverdon, Geoffrey Bridson, Francis Dillon and Michael Barsley for their verbal accounts of their life and times at the BBC. I wish to thank Mrs Linklater for permission to quote from Eric Linklater's *The Cornerstones*, Mrs Butler for allowing me to quote from the writings of Tyrone Guthrie and Faber and Faber Ltd, for allowing quotations from the writings of Louis MacNeice. I also wish to thank the Sieveking family for allowing quotations from Lancelot Sieveking's unpublished memoirs, and to thank Val Gielgud, Donald McWhinnie, W. M. S. Russell, Frances Gray, Eckhard Breitinger, Horst Priestnitz, Rudiger Imhof, John Gielgud and John Braidwood for permission to quote from their works. I am also grateful to the Arts Council of Great Britain for providing me with financial support in the research and writing of this book.

1.
National Responses to Radio

On 13 December 1901 Marconi transmitted the letter S in Morse Code by radio from Poldhu Cove, Cornwall, to St John's, Newfoundland. His invention was very swiftly adapted to serve the needs of civil and military communication and, within twenty-five years, it was being used throughout the world to broadcast public entertainment and information. The development of public broadcasting has stimulated much study of its social and political consequences but very much less critical attention has been paid to its artistic content. It has not been very widely appreciated that radio required the adaptation of existing literary and dramatic forms of expression and that this requirement stimulated experiments which have subsequently had considerable influence upon recent and contemporary writing, in both the new forms of expression and the traditional literary and dramatic forms. The lack of serious attention so far paid to the artistic contribution which radio has inspired is perhaps understandable. Because its aesthetic exploitation has varied considerably from country to country, the interest of serious literary and drama critics has been deflected and seems to have encouraged the belief that radio can only be regarded as a sociological phenomenon. The political impact which radio has had upon societies throughout the world is certainly deserving of study, but critical attention which has been confined to definitions of its social influence based solely on such aspects has tended to encourage a neglect of its role as a cultural catalyst.

Though the physical and psychological relationship between radio stations and their listeners is the same in all countries, the cultural use of radio has varied considerably. It is not safe to assume, for example, that its artistic exploitation has been limited either to those countries which opted for commercially controlled radio stations or to those which established state monopoly broadcasting systems. Within the group of countries operating state monopolies there has been a variation in emphasis on different forms of entertainment. Such variations may even be noted in countries where the radio monopoly has been presumed to be the reserved mouthpiece of dictatorial governments.

When public radio broadcasting started in the twenties, it was immediately used in much the same manner in all countries to broadcast news and information. This news service was directly controlled and censored in some countries while in others a more subtle form of public deception was practised which favoured trivia and thus excluded serious discussions of matters of real portent. But on either side of the news bulletins, the different national cultures immediately displayed preferences for forms of entertainment which appealed to existing national tastes and interests. It was quickly realised that radio could be used to broadcast live concerts and recordings of music, but the kind of music chosen and preferred varied greatly from country to country. The Italians opted for opera while Radio Wien entertained the Austrians with programmes almost wholly devoted to Strauss waltzes and Mozart. An equivalent cultural indication may be found in the USA, where the oldest surviving programme is *The Grand Ol'Opery*, a programme which is devoted to Country and Western music. It should not be forgotten, however, that very local interests and cultural appetites within a country may sometimes determine variations in regional entertainment. Some of the first plays broadcast were performed by the WGY Players from Schenectady, New York, from 1922 onwards and served a special local cultural need. In Britain, where pioneer commercial stations were replaced by a state monopoly in 1922, there was some preference for ballads and music-hall songs, but a cultural bias similar to that which prevailed in New York determined very early that this new form of communication should be used to transmit drama.

Those who are suspicious of the policies and motivations of state monopoly broadcasting may presume that the decision to broadcast plays in Britain was ordered by a paternalistically minded élite who were dedicated to the notion that radio should be used to educate and improve the minds of its listeners. But this is to neglect the historic cultural preference in Britain for spoken drama as opposed to the dramatic forms of the opera or the cantata. This preference was not merely manifest in the theatres of London's West End. It is arguable that a people who are dedicated to a pragmatic view of life naturally prefer to approach philosophic issues by means of the parables which drama and literature offer. In a country where a cloud may sometimes but not always appear dragonish, any parable of life had best be couched in some ambiguity. Too close an approximation to real life does not appeal to a people whose perception of reality is governed by the firm belief that it is a constantly changing condition.

It is therefore not surprising that while the Viennese used radio to give them Strauss and Mozart, the British chose in 1922 to broadcast an excerpt from Shakespeare's Julius Caesar. It was probably inevitable that when the world's first play specifically written for radio was broadcast in 1923, it should be broadcast from London. This new use of the medium to provide a theatre of the air was soon emulated in other countries and thus provided writers in many languages with a new market for their work. The exact number of radio plays which have been written throughout the world since the twenties is not known but in Britain, where the form became something of a speciality, the number of plays now exceeds 40,000. Bearing in mind the British bias in favour of this form of entertainment, this collection of scripts probably constitutes the largest national archive of radio drama in the world.

It would be foolish to claim that all the plays in this huge archive are worthy of serious critical study. But it has sometimes been the case that plays with no intellectual pretensions have pioneered the use of new technical devices and have then in- spired later work of greater significance. A few plays may now be regarded as classic masterpieces of the genre while others can be seen to have anticipated or inspired subsequent developments in theatre and in film. It has not been widely appreciated that radio not only promoted the creation of a dramatic form peculiar to its limitations and opportunities but also offered some writers an imaginative stimulus which has been the genesis of many developments in recent and contemporary theatre. For many writers who are best known for their work in the theatre and in film the radio studio has been their secret workshop. One of the first writers to be apprenticed in this workshop was probably the American playwright Clifford Odets, who left school at fifteen in 1915 to work for a New York radio station. It was not until 1928, when he had long left radio, that he wrote his first play, but there can be no doubt that his experiences as an announcer and radio actor were formative. Other American writers whose radio apprenticeships have played a significant part in their careers are Irwin Shaw and Arthur Miller, and the film scriptwriters Abe Burrows, Arthur Laurents and Jerome Laurence. In Britain, where the BBC early created a benign climate to encourage writers of very various talent, it would be difficult to name a single well-known playwright who had not at some time worked in radio. Some writers effectively began their careers by selling their first plays to the BBC but others began as radio actors or wrote talks, short stories and documentary features.

The patronage offered by the BBC has not merely been a matter of doling out money to needy beginners. It has provided a climate of encouragement and celebration of the imagination through its employment of some rare talents. Several poets, such as MacNeice, Pudney, Rodgers, Terence Tiller and George MacBeth, have worked as salaried producers and while using radio to exploit the limits of their imagination have encouraged others to do the same. Such people not only stimulated the timid beginner. They formed part of a community which from 1945 became, to use Shakespeare's dedication, the 'onlie begetter' of several literary and dramatic movements and ideas. They and their colleagues were in part assisted by the working conditions and atmosphere which generally exist in a radio studio. In contrast to the social condition which usually prevails in a theatre or film and television studios, there is a sense of community in the radio studio in which producers, actors, technicians and writers collaborate rather than compete. There is a swift and open exchange of ideas in an atmosphere of mutual respect which is not common in the theatre or film and television studios.

This congenial and conducive atmosphere naturally extended to the BBC's canteens and to the surrounding pubs like The George, The Stag and the M. L. Club, which for many years have been the social and artistic equivalents for Les Deux Magots in Paris or The Cheshire Cheese of Dr Johnson's time. In such a milieu the novice could glean encouragement and advice from established actors and other writers and from radio drama producers, whose experience in producing not only plays from the classic repertoire but foreign plays in translation made them encyclopaedic experts on the state and nature of drama all over the world. Given this sphere of patronage and its attendant artistic community it is no wonder that so many contemporary British playwrights began their writing careers in radio. Though Alan Ayckbourne began his writing career as a radio drama producer, Giles Cooper learned his trade as a radio actor. Robert Bolt's first published script was written for BBC's *Children's Hour*, while Alun Owen, who started work as a child actor, wrote his first play for radio. Harold Pinter and Samuel Beckett also owe a great deal to the medium and Tom Stoppard, who was a journalist, began his dramatic career by writing a fifteen-minute radio play. Many other writers in Britain have made use of radio to pay for what Dylan Thomas used to call the grosseries of life and, in so doing, their later work has been subtly influenced. It should not be thought that Thomas, for example, had no prior experience of radio when he wrote his play *Under Milk Wood*. He had previously contributed radio talks and had worked as a radio actor in plays and features written by his fellow poets, Louis MacNeice and W. R. Rodgers.

Radio not only offered employment to poets like Thomas; it provided an opportunity to try out new ideas to respond to its very special requirements. In the twenties, there was this entirely new problem of writing a play for an unseen and unseeing audience and the solution of this problem was to lead to various developments in the theatre and the cinema film. Later, in the fifties, there was a revolution in dramatic diction and structure largely generated in the radio studios as a result of certain reactions to the evidence presented by the portable tape-recorder, which demonstrated to writers the true nature of ordinary speech.

Many interpretations of developments in the recent and contemporary theatre often take little account of the influence which radio has had. Some part of this critical neglect may be due to the emphasis which has been placed upon radio solely as a sociological factor, but from its very beginnings there has been a fairly consistent intellectual prejudice against this newfangled gadget and the mass entertainment which it had to provide. This has led to the assumption that most of what has been written for it is pure dross and, at best, a fit accompaniment for the ironing and the washing up. Asa Briggs quotes a fairly early example of this intellectual disdain when he describes Lord Reith's encounter with an Oxford don in 1927 who was proud to tell him that he never listened to the wireless. This attitude has not yet entirely died away although it is now more the vogue in Britain for such people to be disparaging about television. The persistence of this bias against radio has sadly blinded many intelligent critics as to its importance and has left them unaware of the use which has been made of it by writers of some standing.

In some countries where writers of merit have not enjoyed the kind of access to the medium which the BBC afforded in Britain, such critical disdain may be thought justified. It is easy to be dismissive of the general standard of American radio drama and thus to neglect the work of poets like Archibald MacLeish and the large influence which radio writing was to have on dialogue in the cinema film. In France, where the avant-garde writer has largely been denied access to radio by a severely controlled state monopoly, there has been little radio drama of much significance and the more eccentric and dissident talents have tended to find their outlet in films. The cause of this neglect of radio in France has not been a matter of aesthetic choice but it may well be that the traditional respect afforded by British intellectuals to the French model in artistic and literary matters may have confirmed the presumption that because the French did not evolve a school of radio dramatists there could be little merit in radio writing.

Whether the French example has been the excuse for this critical neglect or not, it has to be recognised that many previous artistic and literary innovations have been greeted with a similar dismissal. It is noteworthy that the advent of any form of entertainment which suddenly enlarges the size of the audience or readership has nearly always evoked hostility from those who regarded themselves as the established arbiters of taste. Like the Elizabethan theatre, which was banned to London's apprentices for fear it would corrupt them, like the eighteenth-century novel which was thought likely to sully the minds of young maidens, radio has been regarded as a potentially depraving influence. The same has also been said, of course, of the cinema film and of television and it is instructive that much more attention has been paid to the possible social corruption engendered by all these new forms of entertainment than to the history of their artistic evolution. It has been thought more proper to debate whether they encourage adolescent violence than to study matters like the development of narrative styles in drama, the socio-political themes concealed by Hollywood script-writers in cowboy films or the effects which radio has had on dramatic dialogue and structure.

It has to be said that this almost wilful neglect of the artistic history of the mass media is to some extent understandable. Any form of entertainment which suddenly enlarges the audience outflanks the position of the established critics. A theatre play may be safely judged within the consensus of a relatively small and select social group but there can be no sense of a shared occasion when a play can leap into the ears of almost anyone who cares to listen. It is easy then to conclude that such a play on radio or television can only be of appeal to the despised mass audience and that it cannot therefore be possessed of any artistic merit. It is not surprising therefore that when radio started, few critics of any standing prophesied that it would ever produce anything of aesthetic value. It is sad that despite the enormous contribution which British writers have since made to the radio drama form, this dismissive attitude has tended to persist.

Quality magazines and newspapers in Britain still give more critical attention to work in the traditional literary and dramatic forms than they give to television or radio. A play presented to a theatre audience of a few hundred will usually receive more critical coverage than a television play seen by ten millions or a radio play heard by a quarter of a million people. It is sometimes argued that a theatre play is likely to contain some fresh and original features worthy of comment but this view ignores the fact that on many occasions these apparent innovations have had their origins in a radio studio.

The mandarin view that radio does not really matter has been strangely persistent. One terrible example of this prejudice is to be found in Cyril Connolly's obituary of Louis MacNeice in the *Sunday Times* in 1963 when he regretted that the author of *The Dark Tower* and *Persons From Porlock* and many other brilliant radio plays and features had wasted so much of his talent and

energy in radio. Connolly presumed that MacNeice should have
devoted himself wholly to the more respected activity of writing
poetry for the page. Though he must have listened on more than
one occasion to one of the poet's plays and features on radio, he
refused to acknowledge in his obituary that MacNeice had made
brilliant use of this miraculous device which allows the poet to
share his mental voyaging with a million minds. If he had been
blessed with a more perfect historical perspective, Connolly
would have remarked that MacNeice belonged to the first
generation of poets to be handed this wonder of the air. But
Connolly was possessed of this intellectual prejudice which
presumes that radio is a waste of time and he could not bring
himself to admit that many of MacNeice's plays are classics of the
radio genre and that his work had already had enormous influence upon the work of younger writers.

It would be unfair, though, to single out Connolly for his
apparent ignorance. His bias against radio was common to many
of his contemporaries and associates and it has to be faced that,
even when radio criticism is given adequate space, those who
wish to proclaim its virtues sometimes find this difficult. The
reception of a radio play is a very personal experience which
cannot be shared. The critic is very conscious of the fact that his or
her judgement may therefore be thought too idiosyncratic or
arrogant. The plays may often be well in advance of prevailing
fashions in the theatre and they may thus be difficult to assess. In
the course of the period of five years when I was radio drama
critic for the *Listener* I have to confess that I made some instant
judgements which with hindsight I would now question.

It was at one time the BBC's custom to provide critics with play
texts which served as an aid to correct quotation of a specific line
but did not actually assist critical appreciation. What appeared to
be of a certain shape on the page did not always seem the same
when it was heard, and those who may now attempt to study
radio plays of the past by reading the scripts should appreciate
that what appears on the page is often an incomplete guide to the
resulting production. Reading the scripts without hearing the
plays is no more to be recommended than the unfortunate
scholarly practice of judging theatre plays from the text without
seeing them on a stage. With the radio play there can be an even
greater loss of understanding, even when the reader is familiar

with studio techniques. Directions as to sound effects or scene changes may be very brief when a writer is working with a producer who is familiar with his or her work and has elected to leave the detail of such directions to conversations in the studios during the course of production. But even when such directions are copious it should be remembered that they are only a literary description leading in the direction of an eventual aural effect. It is also difficult to judge the exact pace and running time of a play on the page. It is, for example, a necessary procedure in the BBC's Drama Script Unit to have plays read and timed so that they may be fitted into the programme schedules. But on one occasion a play which was timed by one reader to last only twenty minutes was correctly timed by another to last one hour. Even those who are experienced in this matter of assessing the pace and timing of a play can sometimes fail to assess running time and the student should therefore be wary of judging radio plays simply by reading them.

Certain writers like MacNeice, who was a very competent producer as well as a poet, have written very detailed instructions which may give the reader some appreciation of the eventual production. But even with such detailed scripts there is a great deal missing from the page. It is important to remember that the dialogue has not been written to be read in silence but to be heard aloud. The plays were often written with specific actors in mind who the author knew would convey a certain presence over and above the words.

This presence can only be appreciated by hearing the original disc or tape. Unfortunately, very few radio plays have yet been published on cassette or discs. The past critical neglect and ignorance of the importance of this work has naturally not encouraged much publication. In the meantime, it is possible to hear some original productions at the BBC Sound Archives or at the British Institute of Recorded Sound. At both these places, facilities are necessarily limited and large numbers of would-be listeners cannot be accommodated in the ideal condition of isolated rather than communal listening. Recognising the present difficulties attending the study of radio plays, it is less the intention in this book to make detailed examinations of selected radio classics than to provide a general account of the way radio has been used by various writers and to identify some of the ways in

which the radio experience has influenced the recent development of drama in other forms. Radio was responsible for a subtle
change in the approach of writers to the problems of composition. It demanded words to be heard on their own. It offered the
dramatist some exciting opportunities but imposed some severe
disciplines. It has sometimes been idly observed that radio may
transport the listener on some imagined voyage into Outer Space
or into the Dark Ages or into some uncharted limbo. But all such
transports, no matter how aided by music or sound effects,
depend upon the right words to cue them. Such transports
require the radio dramatist to be very meticulous. Directions as to
movement of characters and scene changes must be mostly contained within the dialogue but they must never be so obvious as
to become laughable. It is also easily said that radio creates its
own scenery but this observation neglects the fact that such
creation is in the hands of the writer.

The severe code of radio's discipline applies equally to the
writers of popular serials and to those who have written some
of the medium's acknowledged masterpieces. Radio demands
above all a craftsmanship and all those who have written for it
have been made to listen much harder to the structure and sound
of ordinary speech from which example all literature and drama
derives. Any study of recent and contemporary literature and
drama which takes no account of this radio experience can only
be incomplete.

2.
The Conflict between Theatre and Radio

Before the advent of radio, the cinema film and television, the audience for a play was socially limited and culturally homogeneous. The writer for the theatre could and did presume his audience to be possessed in common of certain received opinions and prejudices. This audience with its shared experience of life could be relied upon to appreciate the dimensions of the dilemma of a tragic hero who enjoyed or endured similar options and circumstances. The comedies of Jonson, Farquhar or Molière were not written for a random audience which might include coal-miners, farm labourers or fishermen. It had indeed often been a comic device in the theatre to depict certain social types in the sure knowledge that such people were not likely to form a part of the audience. In other plays, where the comedy served a didactic purpose, a social type well known to the audience is portrayed for their instruction and amusement but once again the joke was very private.

With the arrival of radio as a means of conveying plays to a huge national audience, such private jokes either missed their point or could sound unseemly. There was the obvious opportunity to broadcast plays from the classic repertoire as an educational service but it was not immediately realised that such productions sometimes required an additional education to explain their historical and social context. But long before such general consequences were appreciated and long before the writers wrestled with the problems of writing for this random audience, drama producers and actors were faced with the practical problems of translating the language and manners of the stage to the conditions of this new medium. Some account of this conflict of style between stage and radio may not at first appear relevant to a study of radio writing, but some of the problems encountered by radio drama producers anticipate and illustrate the dilemma which was soon to face the writers.

The idea of using radio to transmit plays in Britain cannot be credited to any one person. There seems to have been a tacit agreement that it ought to be tried but nobody worked out any theories of approach. There was no special drama department established by the BBC at Savoy Hill, London, and people like Eric Maschwitz and Val Gielgud (who was later to become Head of Radio Drama for 30 years), were actually employed by *Radio Times*. Mr Gielgud, like his brother John, had begun his working career as an actor and therefore knew his way around the stage. But when he began producing plays for radio he was, like everybody else, stumbling in the dark of this new theatre of the air. He once recalled the difficulties he faced when he employed the great actor, Henry Ainley, to play Othello.

> In Henry Ainley's mind the studio remained obstinately equated with a super Drury Lane and he pulled out every stop of that magnificent organ, his voice, to such effect that I had to station two 'effects' boys – one at each of his elbows – to withdraw him gently but firmly to a distance from the microphone. His performance was magnificent but it was not broadcasting.[1]

It was fairly easy to know that this theatrical style did not work but it was less easy to find the correct style. The search for a new style of performance was not helped by the theatres whose managements, according to Derek Parker, actively discouraged actors from playing for radio until about 1930. They feared the competition. Mr Gielgud recalls that while it was sometimes possible to persuade the older actors to change their ways, the younger actors tended to be much more resistant. It is likely that they feared that if they were heard speaking in a more natural form, their performances would not commend them to theatre producers, who generally believed that it would be better to record performances on the stage and broadcast them. It was also thought that radio was not worth the trouble, requiring, it seemed, a naturalistic style which was anathema to the stage at that time.

It was also a daunting experience to have to perform to a microphone. Having listened to actors complaining about the lack of a comforting audience, R. E. Jeffrey actually suggested in 1927 that there ought to be a radio studio in which actors would perform to a live audience who would give them 'the solid, palpable sympathy' they demanded. This proposal evoked a splendid rebuke from Sir Barry Jackson, who said that if the BBC really thought realism could be achieved in this way, then lecturers on pond life would have to deliver their talks wearing wading boots and carrying shrimping nets in order to make their words convincing.

Although performance before a live audience was later to become the preferred production style for comedy shows, which inherited and capitalised upon the music-hall tradition, Sir Barry's riposte clearly had its desired effect. Live performances of plays either to a studio audience or recorded in a theatre were rarely tried. But, for many years, the actors found radio a trying business. In 1929, after seven years of radio plays, the BBC Handbook contained an article entitled 'The Problems of the Producer'.

> The actor of ability enters a broadcasting studio with the confidence of long acting experience, often to find that the microphone demands that he start learning all over again. 'Then why use actors?' it has often been asked. It is because they have developed, or are naturally gifted with, a sense of drama, the ability of character portrayal and a voice trained in expression.

But while this article dealt with the alternative of employing anyone off the street to play a part closely resembling their role and status in real life, it still did not define the kind of performance required from those possessed of 'the ability of character portrayal and of a voice trained in expression'. It was to take some years to break away from the traditions of the stage and to establish a style of performance which was more naturalistic and less staid. This struggle by the actors both against and towards a new style that suited the medium was accompanied by a similar search for new forms on the part of the writers. There was obviously a need to write dialogue which was closer to ordinary conversation and which was inimical to the kind of lines which could be declaimed from a stage.

Cecil A. Lewis, who had already written *Pursuit,* one of the first action thrillers for radio, wrote about the differences between radio and the stage in 1929.

> The task of the wireless play-writer differs from that of the stage author because, although in broadcasting limitations of inaudible 'stage business' are very narrow, the limitations of action and mis en scèríe are bounded only by the imagination of the listener himself. The stage author deals in scenes and situations which can be presented to the eye. The wireless author may make use of practically any scene or situation which can be conceived by human thought and imagination.

He also indulged in some accurate prophecy when he went on to observe that a greater knowledge of human psychology than that possessed by the stage playwright would be needed in order to write a brilliant radio play. Although he had chosen to exploit the swift and various changes of scene offered by radio to tell the story of an action thriller, he was yet aware of the potential development of the play in which the action could be heard taking place within the minds of the characters. Lewis's reference to the limitations of action and *mise-en-scène* being bounded by the imagination of the listener is perhaps a reaction to the public response to his play. Though the *Manchester Guardian* of 9 January 1928 had liked the play, many listeners had found its swift changes of scene rather bewildering. It is clear from this that just as the actors and the writers were learning how to use radio, the listeners were also in the process of learning how to listen. Within a few years, the structure of Lewis's fast-moving action thriller was to become an accepted formula and it is very doubtful whether any listener today would find his play hard to follow.

It has to be remembered that at this time most listeners were encased in headphones and that reception of the signal was not always free from atmospheric interference. The meticulous enunciation then practised by news announcers to overcome these difficulties was naturally not suited to the pace of dramatic dialogue. Listening to plays required considerable concentration and it is not surprising that listeners were exhorted to adopt a rather severe regime in order to appreciate them. When the world's first radio play, *Danger* by Richard Hughes, was broadcast in 1923, they were advised not to let their children listen for fear they might be frightened. They were also advised to hear the play in the dark. It was somehow believed that this new drama for an audience which had no eyes could only be appreciated by simulating blindness. It was thought that if people listened to the play in a lighted room they would be distracted by their furniture from imagining the scene being fed to their ears.

Despite all this bizarre advice, the play, which was treated as a kind of stunt rather than as something deserving of intellectual esteem, was very successful. It is further interesting to record that *Danger* was not written by a playwright and that it was the purest accident that it was written at all. Hughes had happened to be in the studios at Savoy Hill when it was discovered that there was a gap in the planned schedules which had to be filled very quickly. Hughes offered there and then to write his play. Under the pressure of this deadline and without time to worry unduly about dramatic structure, he created a form for his play which could not be attempted on the stage. His novelist's mind created a story of three miners facing a crisis in a Welsh coal-mine. The setting could not be convincingly portrayed on a stage and the characters involved insisted upon a naturalism of portrayal which was nothing like the prevailing West End style of acting.

Though the play was occasioned by an accident, it is perhaps not so much of an accident that it should have been written by a novelist. It is required of the novel, as it is of the radio play, that its narrative should transport the reader's imagination to appreciate scenes which may or may not be familiar. When people speak in a novel they do not perform or declaim in the manner of a stage play unless they are cued to do so, as, for example, in Dickens's *Pickwick Papers*. In most novels they speak as if they are being overheard and, when they so speak, they have to be overheard speaking in a manner which is natural to their condition and character. It is perhaps, therefore, not all that surprising that Hughes, the novelist, was the one who pointed the way towards the most effective structure for radio drama in this very first play of all.

The suggestion in *Danger* that the listener is eavesdropping on an actual event has since been utilised in countless radio plays. Improvements in recording sound effects and in styles of acting now make it possible to convey completely the sense of being present at some event. But for a writer like Tyrone Guthrie this approach seemed limiting and false. Guthrie is best known for his work as a producer in the theatre and for his championship of the arena stage. It is not widely appreciated that his work for radio probably influenced his approach to the theatre and that his radio plays constitute an important contribution to the development of modern drama. In 1929 he wrote *Squirrel's Cage* and followed it the next year with *The Flowers Are Not For You To Pick*. In 1931, writing in the BBC Handbook, he declared himself to be totally opposed to the realist approach. 'A faithful transcript of real life is almost inevitably dull and, similarly, it is impossible to get actors to resist the temptations of "making effects" – there is nothing so hard as to play a scene in the key of ordinary speech.'

It might be thought that Guthrie is here reacting like many theatre people of his day against a style of naturalism which was found unacceptable in the theatre. But his plays show that he had other grounds for his objections. He appears to confine his objections to the relatively minor complaint that such plays encouraged the actors to 'make effects' but when he says that a faithful transcript of real life is almost inevitably dull he has clearly in mind the alternative kind of drama which radio also offered and which he pioneered.

Guthrie's radio plays do not pretend that we are listening to an actual event in real life. The characters are social archetypes and they are brought to the ear so that their social and political dilemmas may be discussed. In *Squirrel's Cage,* he presents the dilemma facing a social type whose conditions of life would be familiar and identifiable to most listeners even though they themselves might not live in such a manner.

His squirrel in a cage is a young man called Henry who works in a city office and who is trapped in the daily treadmill of commuting to this tedious work from a London suburb. Henry wants to escape into the wide world and seek adventure but he is chained to his treadmill. The play has six scenes which are separated by five interludes in which the central character is engaged in a rhythmic chorus with the other characters. These

interludes serve both as commentary and summary of the
preceding action and as a means of building up tension. Here is a
piece from Interlude III.

ONE VOICE:	All tickets ready, please.
ALL:	Tickets, please.
THE ONE:	She's late again.
ALL:	Late again.
THE ONE	It simply means I'll have to travel on the 8.10.
ALL:	Travel on the 8.10.
THE ONE:	I do nothing but travel up and down on these suburban trains.
ALL:	Suburban trains.
THE ONE:	Up and down – up and down.
ALL:	Up and down – up and down. Up and down – up. and down.

The one voice then changes the issue to that of whether the
window should be up or down and the chorus builds to a
crescendo which is then stopped abruptly by the blowing of a
train whistle. In the preface to the play, Guthrie wrote:

> There is no narration; scene and interlude follow one another
> without a break. After the end of each episode there should be
> a stroke of a bell, then the scream of a syren, suggesting a rush
> through time and space. The 'scenes' should be played very
> intimately in a rather low key; in contrast to the 'interludes',
> which are to be bold and reverberating, each one working up to
> a thunderous climax.

In his second play, *The Flowers Are Not For You To Pick*, Guthrie
employed much the same device but muted it to serve the more
tragic condition of a young clergyman who is in the act of drowning, having fallen overboard from a ship bound for China. There
is again no narration but the play is prefaced by a short observation on the part of the announcer that it is a popular belief that a
drowning man sees his past life. The sound of the waves is then
heard and we are taken back to the man's childhood. We then
visit succeeding scenes in his life which are punctuated by the
'intervals' of the waves. Guthrie was not content, however, to

use actual recordings of sea waves. He specified the kind of
radiophonic effects which only became really adequate to his
specification in about 1960. The sound, he wrote, should be
complex yet symphonic.

> By its rhythms and tone it may be possible to suggest not
> merely the water in which Edward is engulfed, but the beating
> of the heart, the tumult of fear, the immutable laws and
> irresistible strength of Nature compared with our puny and
> inconstant selves.

These plays anticipated technical devices which the radio
studios could not then provide. His employment of the actors to
engage in an ensemble style of performance also anticipated
some of his later work in theatre production. He also learned
from his radio experience the essential lesson that if a character is
not heard for some time, the listening audience will presume that
he or she has gone away. In a stage play, a character who says
nothing but can be seen by the audience is still a part of the
perceivable action. But in his stage productions Guthrie was
never satisfied with these mute figures. To the bewilderment of
old actor managers like Sir Donald Wolfit he insisted that spear-
carriers should appear to be participating in the action. Actors
like Wolfit who were accustomed to a style of production in
which the central characters claimed the audience's full attention
were dismayed by what they regarded as fidgeting and fumbling
that was likely to distract their audiences. As he had done in
radio, Guthrie required contributions to the dramatic event on
stage from every member of his ensemble. It is sometimes
assumed that Guthrie derived his ideas about arena staging from
the Greek theatre but it must surely be the case that some of his
inspiration came from his experience in writing for actors who
were also masked and who were wholly dependent upon the
word in the arena of radio.

Guthrie's third play for radio, *Matrimonial News*, was also
something of a pioneer work. It exploited the concept of the
stream of consciousness, allowing the audience to hear the
private thoughts of a frustrated and disheartened woman. She
has fallen out with her family and is waiting in a cheap restaurant
to make an assignation with a man whose advertisement in a

Lonely Hearts newspaper column she has answered. Guthrie again uses the device of a very short introductory note which is spoken by the announcer.

'Remember,' says the announcer, 'you are overhearing her thoughts. She is alone.'

Once again the central figure in the play is a social type rather than a character and the interest focuses on her dilemma as a sociological rather than a personal one. Guthrie's approach to radio drama was regarded by some contemporaries as very avant-garde and it is clear that he might have written more for radio if his approach had found more acceptance with people like Val Gielgud.

Shortly after the production of Squirrel's Cage in 1929, Gielgud wrote a series of articles in Radio Times on the subject of radio drama. In one of these articles, he remarked that a great deal of nonsense was in his opinion being currently talked about radio being an abstract medium. He then rebuked some enthusiasts, whom he regarded as misguided, who were in pursuit of the ideal of a radio play composed of purely abstract sounds. Anyone whose craft involves the task of communicating ideas and sense by means of the word would readily agree with him here. The idea that sense can be conveyed by sound alone is impractical. But having made this observation, Gielgud then goes on to link this dismissal of the abstract sound enthusiasts with a rather illogical attack on the work of Guthrie. He wrote that the abstract sound idea is 'only a reductio ad absurdum of a practice which has built more than one radio drama about characters so abstract or so symbolical that they are without sufficient identity to make them interesting'.

He then cites Guthrie's Squirrel's Cage and Lancelot Sieveking's Kaleidoscope as examples of this form. He says that the characters in these plays are only puppets and that the interest of the audience is directed towards the circumstances affecting their lives rather than towards their individual characters. It is certainly the case that the characters tend to be archetypal figures but neither of these plays could be said to be moving towards the play which is based upon abstract sounds. Both Guthrie and Sieveking were attempting to find a dramatic form in which their characters would be easily recognisable to this new random audience which did not necessarily share the private jokes and limited social consensus to be found in the theatre. They chose archetypal figures deliberately. Sieveking, for example, in his *Intimate Snapshots* (1929) wrote a dialogue for a lift conductor at a London Underground station and a charlady at a girls' private school. In his unpublished autobiography he wrote:

> One protagonist argues that life is nothing but a series of meaningless repetitions day after day, year after year, and suggests that somehow men and women should try to escape. His opponent holds that there is no escape from the outward daily repetitions but they are merely a background which doesn't matter.

The protagonists, to use Sieveking's word, certainly engage in a rather artificial debate which is similar to that employed by Guthrie. Their speech is also orchestrated and they do not always speak in a normal manner. Sieveking wrote about this play in this manner: 'In it I, so to speak, *slow-motioned* small pieces of speech in several places, sometimes in order to emphasise the meaning of the words as *words*, and sometimes in order to give them special significance as sound forms.' He admits that this may sound high-falutin, but says that he had in mind that moment of mental contact when people suddenly understand each other not only emotionally but intellectually. Sieveking might have added that he was here trying to present a radio equivalent of the exchange of gestures and looks which can be witnessed at such moments on the stage. But, like Guthrie, he was seeking by such orchestration of speech to extend the dramatic range of expression which had become stereotyped. It must have seemed to Gielgud that these portrayals of social archetypes attended by choric interludes and slow-motion speech were aiming at some purely abstract form.

But far from being attempts at the abstract, they were closer to the much earlier dramatic form of the morality play. It is interesting that at about the same time Brecht, who was also influenced by radio and the cinema film, was writing plays which featured similar archetypal figures who were then involved in a debate about their conditions and their dilemma. It will be suggested later that these developments and the evolution of narrative drama and what Brecht called epic theatre were in some part due to the writer's response to the problems created by the enlargement of the audience in radio and the film. But this response had not the benefit of theories of radio drama. Writers, producers and actors were still finding their way.

This state of affairs naturally did not please the critics. R. D. Charques, a critic for the *Listener*, quoted in *Radio Times* (17 January 1930) Leonardo da Vinci's maxim that all practice must be founded on good theory, and demanded that some clear theories should be evolved in radio drama. He did not offer any theories of his own but he may well have been aware of the prevailing chaos which frequently accompanied drama productions. Sieveking gives a good example of these conditions when he produced a feature programme called *The Wheel of Time* in September 1928. The feature involved three groups of performers. Elsa Lanchester and Harold Scott performed old-time music-hall songs to represent Yesterday, a jazz group represented Today, and Edith, Osbert and Sacheverell Sitwell, with Constant Lambert and William Walton, represented Tomorrow. This last group was to give a performance of Walton's *Façade* but, two days before the performance, Osbert Sitwell gave an interview in the *Morning Post*, in which he said somewhat tactlessly that the reason why British actors and actresses were not as good as their predecessors was that they spent too much time concentrating on becoming ladies and gentlemen instead of worrying about their profession. This remark caused the performers of the Today section to walk out of the studio and Sieveking suddenly had to find substitutes who could not be rehearsed before their performance. To add to this confusion, there were the conditions then prevailing in the studio.

The dramatic control panel, by means of which the producer sat in a separate room and controlled a programme, did not yet exist, and so we were all crammed into No 2 studio, a narrow room on the first floor, and I had to listen through headphones and push people up to the Reiss microphone in its blue gauze box and pull them away, waving and making wild signs, which were not always clearly understood as I walked about among them.

He was not much helped on this particular occasion by the fact that the preceding symphony concert overran its time which meant that he was forced to speed up the performance of *Façade* to avoid it clashing with the time signal provided by Big Ben. He achieved this by standing behind Walton who was conducting and making the orchestra go faster than the composer intended. Such frantic conditions were far removed from earnest debates on theories of radio drama.

But Charques made a telling point when he observed that radio drama producers were trying to cope with two irreconcilable objectives; the aim of bringing theatre within the reach of everybody and the creation of a radio form of drama. He praised the BBC for broadcasting plays by Shakespeare, Chekhov, Ibsen and Strindberg and for giving the nation a hearing of the West End success *Journey's End*. But he felt that such productions were not advancing the discovery of a radio form. He also thought that dramatists writing for radio were not taking sufficient account of the fact that their work could only be heard. He seems to have shared Guthrie's dislke of naturalism and his interest in developing a more formal style. Quoting Pater, that all the arts aspire to a form of music, he suggested that it might be worth while exploiting verbal counterparts to the motifs and rhythms of music. He then referred with approval to the interludes in *Squirrel's Cage* as examples of this verbal imitation of musical form.

It is interesting that Guthrie also envisaged a development of this particular kind. In the BBC Handbook for 1931 (page 189) he wrote:

Writers for broadcasting have up to the present concentrated most of their energies on conveying to the audience a series of mind pictures; but it is doubtful whether the future of broadcast drama lies in this direction and whether it would not be more profitable to explore the purely symphonic possibilities of the medium; to make more use of rhythm in the writing and speaking; more deliberate use of contrasting vocal colour, changing tempo, varying pitch. One feels that it is only by attacking the subject from a symphonic angle is it possible to rid the mind of unwanted literary and artistic conventions.

It is ironic that when Guthrie wrote this, his views on radio drama and his manner of writing plays were already associated in Gielgud's mind with enthusiasts for an abstract form based upon pure sound. Guthrie was to encounter great difficulty in getting subsequent plays accepted for broadcasting and, in consequence, devoted all his energies to the theatre. It is a further irony that his call for the development of what he called the symphonic form was heard not by those producing and writing plays but by those who worked in the Features department after it was established in 1935. The creation of feature documentary programmes demanded the journalistic approach, which is generally free of Guthrie's unwanted literary and artistic conventions. But features producers like Geoffrey Bridson and Francis Dillon, and later MacNeice, were to find themselves faced with the need to present their recorded material dramatically. It will later be seen to what use they put the symphonic possibilities of the medium, which was to have considerable influence on the approach of dramatists after 1950.

In the same article in which he called for the symphonic approach, Guthrie also commented on radio's advantages: 'An imaginative writer can build up a scene by subtle and ingenious word pictures, and for an imaginative listener, he will create illusions infinitely more romantic than the tawdry grottos of the stage.'

This jibe at the stage, where he was to spend the greater part of his very creative life, was not an idle one. He was not happy with the state of the theatre, which he regarded as being riddled with complacency. As a writer for radio, he had already become aware of the magic it could create in the mind of the individual listener. But he was also aware that this magic depended upon a verbal subtlety and ingenuity which had not much place on the stage.

It must also be realised that Guthrie was here taking part in a fierce debate which had broken out between those who supported radio and those who sought to defend the stage. The theatre's supporters generally regarded both radio and the cinema film as catchpenny entertainments serving the low tastes of the mob. In 1929 *Radio Times* had invited Gordon Craig and Compton Mackenzie to fire shots at each other across this artistic divide. Craig held the new medium in total contempt, believing that it could only encourage what he called bad plays. Mackenzie, though a novelist and man of letters, had by that time become a radio fan. He admitted that when broadcasting was started in Britain in 1922 he had also regarded it with fear, aversion and contempt but that, in the interval, he had begun to appreciate its power and possibilities. He had written *Carnival* for radio, and had contributed talks and had read a number of his short stories. Like Guthrie, he had been made aware of its enormous possibilities.

> I have realised that radio is going to give the artist the greatest opportunity he has had since the days of Homer to express himself without the mechanical barrier which the progress of human inventiveness has raised higher and higher between the artist and his audience.

It could be objected here that Mackenzie's rhetoric overlooks the fact that radio was one of the products of human inventiveness and that it provided some new barriers of its own making but he was already aware, from his own experience, of the immediate communication between the individual artist and the private imaginations of the millions at their firesides. Craig somewhat predictably had no time for this millenial stuff about Homer's second coming and feared only that radio might keep some potential theatre-goers at home and thus lower box office receipts. Craig does not come out well in this debate and it might be thought, too, that Mackenzie exaggerated in his enthusiasm.

But the reference to the conditions which Homer enjoyed is apposite in another way. It is perhaps rather obvious to state that radio requires an author to write his words to be heard and not to be read in silence. But this obvious requirement is underestimated in critical approaches to the work of writers who have been influenced by radio since the twenties. For apart from the problems created for the dramatist and the debate which waged between those who favoured naturalism and those who favoured some new form like the symphonic, radio restored a manner of composition which, as Dr W. M. S. Russell has pointed out, was the commonplace of ancient literature. The writer had once again to match his words, even in a broadcast talk, to the natural cadence and manner of his normal speech. In a lecture on 'The Sound Drama of Seneca', Dr Russell said:

Virtually all ancient Greek and Roman literature was designed to be read aloud. Studio performance was the normal method of publication. Even if you read in private, you read aloud to yourself. St Augustine mentions as a prodigy a man who actually read books in silence; visitors came to watch this amazing man reading. Busy people sometimes had new books read to them by a servant. Sound was of the essence. Things were not all that different for the Elizabethan and Victorian middle classes. The Elizabethan yeoman's son would read a new book to him and the Victorian father read aloud to his family. The growing prevalence of silent reading may help to account for the lack of music and rhythm in so much modern prose.[2]

It may certainly be true that much of the tortuous prose which serves bureaucracy and some scholarship today has been created by writers who have never tested their composition by reading it aloud. It is also the case that some literary critics have arrived at inappropriate conclusions when dealing with Irish drama and literature, in particular, where the tradition of what I must call oral composition did not die out as it did in England in the 1880s. In Irish literature it has always been a necessity to hear the words as well as read them silently on the printed page. This necessity must now apply to other writers in English whose approach to composition has been affected by the presence of radio.

The presumption that radio can only offer a second-hand form of theatre for the mass audience or that it can at best serve serious novelists as a means of advertising their work tends to obscure the use which many writers have made of it and the way in which their styles of expression have been changed and affected by using it. Novelists like Mackenzie and E. M. Forster were early contributors of talks and short stories and there is no doubt that their style was altered by this writing to be heard. But the full consequences of this formative influence were not to be witnessed until some of the younger writers, whose careers actually began with radio work, had worked their way from its studios to the novel, the stage and the film. It was to create a climate which was later to bring about a revolution in dramatic diction and structure and it was to aid and improve the quality of film dialogue.

But before these general influences were felt, the pioneers who stumbled in this new darkness had to deal with more immediate problems. It is interesting that during the same period, the pattern of development was somewhat similar in Germany. The Germans began by using the microphone to eavesdrop on what was essentially a theatrical performance. They then improved studio techniques and neglected dramatic content and quality in the pursuit of utilising these techniques. They then realised that they had blundered and that the only answer was a play of distinction which yet took account of the very particular conditions in which it was to be produced and heard. Writing in *Radio Times* for 28 August 1931, Brabazon Howe, a radio drama producer, reported this German story with some amazement. He no doubt presumed that the Germans would have worked close to some considered theory instead of blundering about as he and his British colleagues had done. He was forced to conclude that the Germans had done no better.

We are accustomed in this country to admitting as an axiom that, certainly as far as things theatrical are concerned, development has always come from abroad, and that the West End theatre is thinking today what Berlin or Moscow thought in 1907. But oddly enough, as far as the broadcast play is concerned, England seems to lead the field.

In these early years of radio it is true that, in the field of the broadcast play, British broadcasting was very successful. Drama producers had tactfully restrained their actors from pitching their voices up as if they were still in the theatre. The writers had pursued a new kind of naturalism which was sometimes made to sound absurd because the sound effects which accompanied their words had to be manufactured in the studios. This naturalism had also been disliked by writers like Guthrie whose work pointed towards a totally new development of dramatic expression which was only possible in radio. But there were some other responses to the radio problem which were pioneered elsewhere, in Germany and the USA. The evolution of narrative drama was more particularly a German and American interest which was also to have subsequent effects on work in the theatre and in film.

3.
The Need for Narration

A form of drama in which a narrator is used overtly to describe changes of scene and relevant information which is not contained within the dialogue is thought by the purist and by the dramatic craftsman to be the lazy way to write a play. Julian MacLaren Ross, who was later to make some brilliant adaptations of novels for radio, put this point well when he first made contact with the BBC in April 1938, when submitting his play *Gallows Alley*. He wrote to Moray McLaren:

> I have listened to many plays on the air and it seems to me that, while some of them achieve a very high standard, the full possibilities of the medium have not yet been exploited. For example, it should not be necessary for the announcer to out-line the scene where the play is being enacted, or for stage directions to be read aloud; everything should be conveyed to the listener by means of sound and dialogue.[1]

MacLaren Ross was writing at a time when broadcasters and listeners had acquired some familiarity and sophistication and were therefore ready to dispense with narrative drama. But in the early days, the narrated play had served a necessary social purpose. For, despite grand nationalistic claims to cultural sophistication, theatre-going in most countries in the twenties was the recreation of a very small social élite. Experience of drama was otherwise limited to attending amateur performances and the music-hall or vaudeville. The potential range of drama which could now be offered via radio, a range which was later to include everything from Greek tragedy to contemporary foreign theatre and radio plays in translation, was an invitation which had to be approached with some caution. The new mass audience had limited experience of the theatre and was still in the process of learning how to listen.

In many countries the form which immediately seemed to offer the best chance of being easily understood and received was that of the narrative play or dramatised story. This form allowed the presence of a narrator who could take the listeners by the hand and lead them into and out of the dramatic action.

It may be thought that this dramatic form was wholly an invention of radio but its style and structure have their origins in the novel in the days when novels were written to be read aloud. It was an embellishment of the style of Dickens, who used to give public readings of his novels; offering the added pleasure of dialogue performed by a group of actors and not by a single voice. It was adopted not merely to present a single play or story but to present serial drama of the kind which became extremely popular in the USA. It was employed in Britain to present dramatisations of popular and classic novels, whose narrative style almost dictated this form of adaptation, and it was developed in Germany by the socially committed dramatists like Brecht who argued that drama should instruct and not merely entertain.

It has to be remembered that when radio started, broadcasters in all countries, whether the radio stations were state-controlled monopolies or run by commercial enterprises, faced a common problem in varying degrees when they began to transmit plays. Even in countries with a supposed common heritage and language and a nationhood going back many centuries, the play which had appealed to and pleased a relative minority might cause offence to or be misunderstood by certain sections of the nation. Although in Britain the BBC under Lord Reith was early devoted to the belief that radio should be used to educate and inform the mass audience, it had constantly to guard itself against accusations of mandarinism and metropolitan bias. In the USA there was a far more pressing need to provide forms of dramatic entertainment for an audience which had far less cultural homo-geneity than any nation state in Europe.

In his survey of the impact of radio and television on human societies, Marshall McLuhan arrived at the conclusion that the new media would ultimately replace print as the major form of communication. He seems to have based this conclusion upon his observation of what appeared to take place in the USA in the twenties and thirties. It appeared to him that people were reading less and less and listening more and more.

But this is to leave out of account the fact that in European countries like Britain and Sweden and Germany the radio actually stimulated listeners to go and read classic novels or to visit the theatre. It is also to ignore the fact that, for many Americans in the twenties and thirties, English was not their ancestral tongue. This was a period when newspapers in Polish or Swedish, for example, were flourishing; indicating that though the mass of the population might not be reading Emerson in English, it had not lost the reading habit entirely. The various nationalities who formed a part of the Melting Pot sometimes preferred to read the language of their origins. Such people were often proficient in colloquial English while their elders still tended at home to speak their native tongues.

The task of serving the polyglot population with information and entertainment was left entirely to commercial radio stations, whose primary objective was not educational but the economic need to attract the optimum number of listeners to satisfy those who sponsored programmes and paid for advertising. It was inevitable that the broadcasters had to devise systems of entertainment and information which would appeal to the greatest number. It is to their credit that they succeeded so well and thus created the impression that radio was actually superseding the more ancient communication of print.

A colloquial style was vital and the kind of English spoken by an educated Briton was thought suspect and high-falutin. This reaction was succinctly expressed by a film distributor in the USA who did not take to Alexander Korda's British-made film, *Things To Come*, when he said: 'Nobody is going to believe that the world is going to be saved by a bunch of people with British accents.'[2] American radio had to avoid the mandarin style of presentation and, in order to please the sponsors and advertisers, it also had to avoid topics which might invite acrimony or political debate. During an era when American theatre was displaying a fair degree of social and political commitment, when Eugene O'Neill was writing *The Emperor Jones* (1928) and Clifford Odets, radio's first apprentice, was writing *Waiting For Lefty* (1935), radio drama was generally confined to situation comedy and family serials.

Eckhard Breitinger has pointed out that sponsored radio was
bound to encourage these particular forms to the exclusion of
others.

The advertising message and the sponsored programme had to
be matched in intention, execution and style. A sponsor would
certainly not pay for a programme that deviated distinctly in
its argument or style from his sale or promotional interests.
Advertising message and programme message had to be
mutually supporting so that the listener automatically
associated the brand name with the sponsored programme
and vice versa. As a consequence, the programme must be
instantaneously recognisable by the use of stereotyped voices,
settings, situations and uniformly repetitive plot patterns.
Sponsoring almost inevitably entails formula drama. Commercial sponsoring and commercial forms of production
also entail market and product analysis and promotional
campaigns, such as the give-aways which became a regular
feature of serials in the early thirties. It also implies an
implementation of industrial modes of manufacturing scripts
by using dialoguers and the almost mechanical assembling of
individual scenes or parts of a programme by different hands
into a 'unified' whole.[3]

Such factory conditions obviously precluded the free expression of the individual artist and rarely encouraged work of
intellectual integrity. But even if commercial interests had not
played such a large part in determining the standards of
American radio, the narrated play would still have been a
necessity. Its random and disparate audiences required a genial
interlocutor to lead them into the dramatised scenes. They
required plays containing easily appreciated stereotyped
characters who did not advertise differences which might
identify them with particular locales or racial groups. The
duologue serial *Amos n' Andy*, which began in Chicago in 1928
and derived from the newspaper comic strip, became one of the
most popular shows in the history of American radio but it
eventually aroused the anger of black Americans.
It therefore has to be faced that bland and inoffensive entertainment was a social as well as a commercial necessity. The

factory conditions attending the manufacture of scripts in a 'unified' style obviously provided little place for the free expression of the individual artist but it should not be thought that American radio was incapable of some occasional moments of genius and that writers of integrity were always barred. In 1936 at CBS, Irving Reis initiated poetic drama on radio when he invited Archibald MacLeish to write *The Fall Of The City*. MacLeish opted for the narrative form and is credited by Erik Barnouw with establishing this form. Although his poetic narrative has distinct literary merit, it was clearly a form which was already in use, and what is more important about MacLeish's contribution is that it awakened serious writers to the opportunities of the medium. 'The eye is a realist,' MacLeish wrote, 'the ear is already half a poet.' In the preface to his play, he appealed to his fellow poets to make use of radio, which 'had developed tools which could not have been more perfectly adapted to the poet's uses had he devised them himself'.[4]

MacLeish's play told in blunt terms a parable of this time of dictatorships in which the people await a tyrant to lead them. The masked leader is accepted by them and takes power but, when unmasked, is found to be hollow and faceless. The play gained instant acclaim and encouraged some equally adventurous work from others. Orson Welles, who had played the radio announcer in *The Fall Of The City*, produced a version of *Julius Caesar* which employed a historical narrative comment taken from Plutarch, who was played by H. V. Kaltenborn, whose voice was already well known as a radio news commentator. In some other productions, Welles played the narrator and in 1938 he produced Howard Koch's adaptation of *The War Of The Worlds* by H. G. Wells. This production has some notoriety because it conveyed the immediacy of a combat report from a war correspondent and actually convinced many listeners that some form of inter-planetary war had actually broken out.

It may be thought that Koch departed from the conventions of formula drama and that MacLeish invented a new form of narrative play. But in fact they exploited the existing conventions rather in the manner of the screenplay writers in the fifties who utilised the formula of the cowboy picture to convey political messages. From 1936, when the civil war in Spain awakened Americans to the likely dangers of an impending conflict in

Europe, the radio audiences had also become more sophisticated and were prepared to listen to language that was richer and more heightened than they had heard in the past. They were ready for some good rhetoric which was a match for the hard realities they were hearing from radio correspondents like Kaltenborn. But the effects of this intervention on the part of artists of integrity were to be felt less in subsequent American radio than in the film.

American radio writers made a very significant contribution to the style and development of film dialogue. Their listeners and their employers had demanded a style of speech which was very close to that of ordinary conversation. When the Movies first became Talkies in 1928, the film-makers do not seem to have immediately realised that dialogue required some craft. The silent film had created some grand illusions which were unsullied by speech. The containment of essential dialogue to the printed slide had encouraged an acting style in which intentions and emotional reactions were mimed and which further enhanced a sense of mystery and ambiguity. All these illusions were shattered when the actors could be heard mouthing banalities and employing the kind of delivery which was then the norm in the theatre. In the very early days of Talkies, these infelicities were largely set aside. There was a huge market demand for musical comedy which could be easily heard on cinema loud-speakers and which only required rather theatrical dialogue between the musical set pieces.

But when the film-makers turned towards the problem of presenting portraits of real life they faced some of the difficulties which the radio people had been working with for many years. Radio writers had not merely learned to imitate ordinary speech. They had learned that the ear, when presented with a medley of sounds emanating from a single speaker, does not always easily discriminate. They had learned that the circumstances of a scene had to be cued in advance, that the next speaker must be similarly cued. It was not enough to present a perfectly recorded piece of actuality; the listener had to be told what was happening. It had been learned that naturalism had to be concocted and that narrative drama was one of the ways in which this could be done. They had also learned to use the perspective of moving actors to and from the microphone to create the sense of movement.

The relevance of the radio experience to film-making was not immediately appreciated. The grand epoch of the silent film had created the belief that the film was not a dramatic form requiring literary talent but some kind of mobile relative of the plastic arts which could only be moulded by the director. The writers of dialogue were at first employed rather in the manner of verbal plumbers to supply aural versions of the printed slides. But as time passed the radio apprenticeship became an important factor in the careers of many successful screen-writers. Arthur Laurents, who wrote the screenplays for *The Snake Pit* (1948), *Rope* (1949), *Anna Lucasta* (1949), *Bonjour Tristesse* (1955) and *Anastasia* (1956), wrote radio plays between 1943 and 1945. Abe Burrows, who also started in radio, wrote *Guys and Dolls* (1950) and *The Solid Gold Cadillac* (1956), while the team of Jerome Lawrence and Robert Edwin Lee, who directed WHK-WCLE radio at Cleveland, Ohio, from 1937 to 1938, were to write the screenplays of *Inherit The Wind* (1955), *Auntie Mame* (1957) and *A Call On Kuprin* (1961). Robert Anderson, who wrote *Tea And Sympathy* (1953) and *All Summer Long* (1954) and the screenplay of *The Nun's Story* (1959), also started in radio.

Some of the lessons which radio had taught could not easily be applied in the cinema. Though the experience of watching a film is private and may be compared to the condition of listening to radio, cinema sound equipment has remained a very blunt instrument. The kind of sound perspectives achieved in radio long before the invention of stereophony cannot be emulated in the cinema where the sound has to overcome the presence of the audience. In films, all oral exchanges, whether in close-up or whispered aside or shouted from horseback in the Nevada Desert, have to be conveyed at nearly the same sound level.

When Welles made *Citizen Kane* in 1941 he tried to overcome this lack of sensitive sound balance by importing various radio techniques. He naturally had a narrator but also indulged in the device of other commentaries on the action, sometimes in the form of the aside. But the conditions of reception in a cinema effectively blunted these refinements. Though the vision is private in the cinema, the sound is very public and cannot allow the subtleties of radio's aural range. But some of the manners of *Citizen Kane*, which derived from Welles's radio experience, were to become part of film style. The crime film, with the speech-over narrative employed to convey the sense of recalling a real event in someone's life, owed much to the radio style of the narrative drama.

The commercial pressures which created the factory product of formula drama in the USA, and which required an easy vernacular narrative to attract and hold the listeners, did not apply in British or German radio. But the narrated play was fostered in both these countries in response to somewhat different social and political objectives. In Britain, the accepted principle that radio should serve education meant that the daily programmes for children, entitled *Children's Hour*, had to inform as well as entertain. One of the monuments of these British programmes in the thirties was the work of L. du Garde Peach, who devoted himself to the retelling of national history for radio. In Germany, in the days of the Weimar Republic before Hitler came to power, it was the socially committed theatre led by Bertholt Brecht which took the view that drama should instruct rather than merely entertain. Working in a period when radio and the cinema film were determining and suggesting the form of narrated drama, Brecht was later to recall this change of emphasis in the theatre. 'Suddenly the stage began to narrate. The narrator no longer vanished with the fourth wall.'[5]

The movement on the part of L. du Garde Peach towards the creation of the narrative play for children does not appear to have been moulded by any preconceived theory of approach. He began his career by writing short dramatic sketches for BBC Belfast in 1927. In 1928 he experimented with the compilation of ballad operas, which significantly involved the use of narrative.

The first of these works was *Up The River*, which was devoted to the life and times of Shakespeare, and he followed this with *London's a-Calling* and *True History of Henry VIII*. Intended for adult audiences, these ballad plays did not seek to teach or retell history but served to confirm the accepted legends of a Merrie England. But in 1932 he turned away from supplying comforting stories from the past and towards matters of more immediate social and political concern. In the midst of the world economic depression he wrote *Bread*, which told the family history of some people who were, with rather heavy point, called Burden. The play's theme was man's continuing inability to ensure a balance between production and distribution. It began with the Burden family leaving England for America in the 1840s following the repeal of the Corn Laws, which caused a depression in British agriculture. The Burdens become American wheat-farmers and the play ends with their descendants facing the crisis of depression in the USA. This didactic work was followed by *A Pageant Of The Tower,* which told the story of the Tower of London, and by the first dramatisation in any form of the story of *The Mutiny On The Bounty.* In 1933 du Garde Peach wrote *Three Soldiers,* which was about three ex-First World War soldiers on the dole. He seems to have been encouraged by the reception of this play to try another topic of immediate moment. But *Gold,* which analysed the crisis of inflation and the role of the gold market, fell foul of that indefinable censorship which sometimes afflicts the BBC. It was postponed for six months on the grounds that it was thought too controversial.

It is not clear whether this experience diverted du Garde Peach from writing plays on contemporary subjects but from this time he devoted himself to writing history plays for children. In series like *The Castles Of England,* in which a historical figure associated with the particular castle generally told the story, he took his young listeners through the history of their country. So that the events dramatised could be carefully explained in their historical context, the narrative form was a necessity. As with the American audiences, this children's audience needed the narrator to instruct and set the scene.

These history plays also played their part in preparing the ground for a change in dramatic diction. The prevailing theatrical convention still regarded the history play as a costumed pageant. To comport with this pageant style it was thought proper that historical figures should use archaic forms of speech of a pseudo-Elizabethan kind. Despite the fact that Shakespeare had used the language of his day in his history plays, the use of the modern idiom was disliked. But on radio and for a child audience all this 'tushery' and 'by my halidom' was completely out of place. Du Garde Peach had to write speeches which were neither so strange and archaic as to be laughable nor so embellished as to be incomprehensible to his audience. His diction therefore had to move closer to everyday contemporary speech and it thus prepared the way for a treatment of history which was not dressed in fustian language.

The narrative drama of L. du Garde Peach was evolved in

response to perceived needs and practical experience but the dramatic style espoused by Brecht in Germany had a much more deliberate purpose and theoretical basis. In his essay *Theatre For Learning*, Brecht recalled the ideas and conditions which led to his creation of what he called the epic theatre. He acknowledges the influence of Alfred Döblin, the novelist and essayist, who first championed the epic style in contrast to the Aristotelian style of drama. But he also makes the point that this style of drama had suddenly become more practical to present on the stage because various technical improvements in stage machinery, lighting, projection and film made it possible to move the action more swiftly. These technical improvements coincided with an age in which 'the most important human events could no longer be so simply portrayed as through the personification of driving forces or through subordinating the characters to invisible, metaphysical powers'.[6] The role of the environment had to be shown as bearing upon the central character as an independent element. The epic form allowed the theatre to instruct, to lay bare by exposition the issues which faced the characters, to demonstrate the alternatives being offered.

Brecht continues: 'The theatre entered the province of the philosophers – at any rate, the sort of philosophers who wanted not only to explain the world but to change it. Hence the theatre philosophised; hence it instructed.' The philosophy principally involved here was Marxism and it is very easy to associate the epic style solely with Brecht and this particular philosophy. But as we have seen, the form which Brecht adopted so successfully was not limited to his theatre of learning. Variations of it, with very different social and political objectives, are to be found in Britain and America where the problems created by radio invited this style of drama. It may not seem right to compare Brecht's epic theatre with that of the formula drama of American radio but both these forms sought to instruct in their different ways. The plays of Guthrie, who does not seem to acknowledge the inspiration of Brecht's example, also employed many of the devices to be found in Brecht's plays. For he too employed archetypal figures in conflict with their environment and its society and he also exploited the device of the choric commentary.

It is understandable that Brecht should attribute the evolution of his theatre of learning wholly to the social exigencies and political debates which so totally preoccupied Germany in the twenties and that he should trace the ancestry of his inspiration solely to Döblin. But like the characters in his plays, Brecht was himself a man of his time seeking ways in which to respond to his predicament. Like many writers tracing the genealogy of their inspiration, he acknowledged only those influences which seemed immediate to his particular interest, but the structure of his plays also suggests another possible influence with very special German traditions. The structure of many of Brecht's plays recalls the dramatic structure of Bach's cantatas. The cantata also contains the recitative, the solo voice counterpointed by choric responses and the final resolving chorale. In *The Threepenny Opera*, Brecht has the *schluss chorale* deliberately announced in a manner which makes satirical reference to the cantata tradition. In his *St Joan Of The Stockyards* (1928), which was given a brilliant radio production in Britain in 1961 by H. B. Fortuin, the pattern of statements and responses, ending with the final coda of a chorale statement, also suggests the influence of the cantata form.

To draw attention to the fact that Brecht's theatre of learning was heir also to the dramatic traditions of the cantata and to point out that he was not alone in his day in pursuing the narrative play is not to minimise his work or to detract from his achievement. When the stage suddenly began to narrate in the Weimar Republic, drama elsewhere was also turning to this form. Brecht's theatre was most certainly different from the theatres of London and Paris and New York. Outside the fierce climate of debate and innovation which typified the German theatre in the twenties, other theatres were not disposed in the same way to become arenas of social and political polemic. Apart from the political hostility towards the obvious message his plays contained, there was also an aesthetic prejudice in favour of the Aristotelian form. It was to take nearly thirty years for Brecht's work to reach the British stage and it is relevant that, apart from the advocacy of critics like Kenneth Tynan, the movement urging the presentation of his plays was led by people who had worked in radio. Some of those who campaigned for his plays to be performed shared his political views but it is important to realise that some did not. The epic form is often associated only with Brecht's political view but it was a form which lent itself very specially to radio's conditions. It was a form which, for example, David Jones later utilised to great effect while proclaiming somewhat different philosophical motives. Jones declared that his purpose was 'the showing forth of our inheritance'. It should be clear that the narrative drama, whether it took the epic form prescribed by Brecht or the style of children's history plays by L. du Garde Peach or the poetic drama of MacLeish or the formula drama pattern of sponsored radio in the USA, was inspired and predicated by radio. Public broadcasting, as opposed to the relatively private social event of the theatre, involved entertaining a random audience which needed instruction and guidance.

It could well be concluded that the shape and structure of drama was determined by radio and that this development argues that the medium in some way shaped the message it carried. But this is to ignore the way in which different cultures adapted their approach to the creation of the narrative form. Radio initiated an age of instruction in which the people, as in MacLeish's play, looked for a hero to lead them. It became one of the principal agents of political persuasion in Hitler's Germany but it should not be thought that because it was so obviously manipulated by the Nazis in the thirties it did not serve similar purposes of social instruction elsewhere. In entertainment, it had to be so used. In drama, it was not safe to assume that all the listeners shared the kind of shared received opinions which characterised theatre-going audiences. The play's story had not merely to be told; its circumstances and context had to be explained. In some cultural contexts, this explanation was deliberately polemical and didactic while in others the instruction was less apparent. But however the form was used or abused, it invited the artist to take up a position relative to the new huge audience which Compton Mackenzie had compared to that once enjoyed by Homer. Radio required the theatre of learning and its audiences needed the narrative intervention.

4.
The Revolution in Diction

The evolution of dramatic structures which were peculiarly suited to radio and its audiences was later to influence dramatic structures in the film and the theatre. But radio's need to provide entertainment for the mass audience also required a style of literary and dramatic diction and of performance which was closer to the idiom of ordinary speech. It could not support a style of diction which was too refined or socially remote. The caricatures of demotic speech which had satisfied and amused the mandarin consumers of *belles-lettres* and socially exclusive theatre plays were not acceptable to the mass of listeners, most of whom spoke various forms of the demotic. When radio started in countries like Britain it was not immediately realised that this new form of entertainment and information required voices with whom the mass of listeners could easily identify and associate. Radio argued logically that writers wishing to depict Durham miners or unemployed dockers in Liverpool should represent their idiom and dialect with some accuracy and understanding and that actors should perform such speech with insight and respect.

But in Britain this revolution in diction and presentation was to take many years to overcome certain social and artistic prejudices and it was not finally achieved until the fifties. It was a revolution which owes much to the example of radio and to the people who worked in it. In the USA such a revolution was quite unnecessary. American social and political history had already determined that social distinctions should not be based upon the usage of patrician or demotic speech. Though there was a convention which allowed comic imitations of black American speech from the southern states, as used in *Amos n' Andy* and *The*

Black and White Minstrel Show, it was not the practice to burlesque or caricature the speech of white Americans. In responding to market pressures to attract the maximum number of listeners, American radio could not presume any one dialect of American English to be inferior or superior to another and had to encourage the voices of all to be heard as equals. The fact that for technical reasons it had to be transmitted on a regional basis and not from capital cities, as in Europe, meant also that it had to encourage the use of provincial and local voices.

This exposure of the many various dialects of American English did not lead to any kind of revolution in diction on the part of American writers. It may have helped occasionally to improve their ear for the language but it could not be said that novelists like Steinbeck or Hemingway were persuaded to modify their style in response to what they heard on the radio. They were already heirs to a tradition which celebrated the rhythms and patterns of ordinary and not necessarily cultivated speech. This tradition had already trained the American writer's ear to heed the music of demotic speech. Both Hemingway and Steinbeck write as if they are sitting or walking beside their characters and do not presume to be detached patrician observers patronising the people in their stories. Steinbeck's dialogue is often so close to real speech that the reader may actually hear the sound of their voices beyond the printed page. His cowboy vagrants and casualties of the Depression years may be presented to each other as comic or absurd but they are not so presented to the reader. Steinbeck achieves this effect because his close observation of their living conditions and of their speech manners is faithful and accurate and never an exercise in caricature.

It is instructive that while Steinbeck could achieve this sense of realism, some of his British contemporaries failed to do the same because they were working within a different literary and social tradition. An American might comment that this tradition was partly the creation of that feudalistic division into patrician and demotic which the Revolution set aside in 1776. British literary and dramatic convention presumed that matters of moment and of serious concern could only be discussed in the patrician style and voice and that the demotic was an inferior language only spoken by simpletons, social inferiors and comic characters.

Serious study of the demotic and of those who spoke it could be permitted under the heading of folklore studies but the writer was not supposed to bring such people alive on the stage. When Synge wrote *The Playboy of The Western World* he earned the regret of Lady Gregory. Instead of the play, she would have preferred him to continue bringing back 'tales of faery' from western Ireland which could be graciously admired for their quaintness. It was a part of this tradition to represent the demotic by employing phonetic spelling which was usually only an approximation.

This kind of approximation often failed to record accurately the exact vowel sounds or elisions of speech and, being intended more as a superficial hint that dialects were being spoken, British writers often failed to come as close to the real idioms as their American contemporaries did. In *Sons and Lovers*, for example, D. H. Lawrence employs the phonetic device to indicate the speech of Nottinghamshire coal-miners but his representation of their speech is curiously tone-deaf. Though he actually came from Nottinghamshire, he demonstrates little of that understanding of speech rhythms which typifies Steinbeck's knowing command of syntax and sentence form. It was far from his intention to present his characters as comic figures or caricatures but he was, even so, unable to portray their speech as it really is. It so happens that this particular regional speech was better represented by George Eliot in her *The Mill On The Floss* and *Middlemarch*. Unlike Lawrence, she does not resort to phonetic spelling and apostrophes and is one of the exceptions to the patrician tradition which Lawrence, despite his origins, adhered to.

The British theatre in the twenties and thirties naturally reflected this same tradition. It was presumed that the captains and the kings had to deliver their speech in the approved patrician dialect of Oxford English. The portrayal of servants, members of the urban working classes and rural people was undertaken by employing roughly three accepted approximations of dialect. There was something called Cockney, for example, which the trained ear may note is capable of considerable variation within the area of London but which was used very indiscriminately to depict any member of the working class in south-east England. For rural characters, whether they hailed from Norfolk or Somerset, or from Buckinghamshire, as is the case with Dogberry and Verges, there was an accepted stage dialect known as Mummerset. The third accepted form of speech in the theatre was Northern, which was full of 'ee bah gums' and was mainly used as a comic device. This Northern speech form took little account of the enormous differences between the speech of Liverpool and that of the Yorkshire West Riding or even Tyneside and it was sustained by the southern patrician notion that anyone living north of the River Trent was either vulgar or comic or both. The climate of opinion which this style of representation reflected undoubtedly explains the slow and grudging acceptance of a novelist like J. B. Priestley, whose novels dared to chronicle the lives and thoughts of Yorkshiremen as if they were deserving of serious attention.

It was inevitable that when state monopoly radio started in Britain, and also in France, the voices employed to read the news had to speak the patrician dialect of Oxford English, and, in the case of France, that of cultivated Parisian. The notion that matters of state could be described in the speech of Leeds or Bristol was unthinkable. It was even hoped by some of those who regarded the new medium wholly as an agency of education that in the course of time the whole population would learn from the example of the announcers how to speak the tongue which they regarded as correct English. Such people were quite unaware in their social isolation of the fact that Oxford English was regarded as a huge joke.

In radio comedy shows in Britain during the thirties and forties there was a popular and persistent gag which poked fun at the haughty voices of the readers of the news and the weather forecasts. Dennis Gifford, who composed a series entitled *Laughter In The Air*, dealing with radio comedians (1979), made the point that this rather banal joke had continuous success because the comedians were at that time the only regular broadcasters who did not speak in the patrician dialect. Comedy allowed and encouraged the demotic dialects and the comedians who took care to employ the speech of their origins could always raise a laugh from their studio audiences and from the mass of listeners by imitating the restrained speech of Oxford English.

It was not until 1941, when it was thought that a regional voice might give greater credence to the bulletins, that Wilfred Pickles, a Yorkshireman, was allowed to read the news. While many welcomed this break with tradition, there were others who were deeply shocked, maintaining that Yorkshire speech rendered serious matters laughable. This view was not shared by people like Archie Harding, who had begun the long battle to get the voices of ordinary people heard on radio in 1933.

Harding, who was an Oxford graduate with Marxist persuasions, had begun his radio career producing plays in London. In 1932 he produced and compiled a Christmas Day programme which was the first to link speakers from the various Commonwealth countries and which ended with a message from King George V. The programme was an instant success and he was immediately asked to compile a similar programme linking the countries of Europe. This was generally well received but the Polish government took exception to references to the amount it was spending on armaments. Harding was admonished and was removed to what was then regarded as the British equivalent of Siberia. He was put in charge of feature programmes in Manchester. D. G. Bridson, the producer and poet, who began his radio career under Harding's tutelage, has described Harding's views at that time.

> All broadcasting, he insisted, was propaganda; because it did not attack the anomalies of the capitalist system, it became propaganda in tacit support of them. Average people everywhere were painfully inarticulate; but how much less articulate than most were the average people here in the North? As he saw it, that was hardly an accident. For where economic collapse had brought the people so much hardship, continuance of the system required that the people should remain unheard. As part of the system itself, he maintained, the BBC had been careful to see that they did.
>
> In Harding's view *all* people should be encouraged to air their views, not merely their professional spokesmen. And that went for the Working Class no less than for the Middle and Upper Classes.[1]

Bridson comments that one did not need to be a Marxist to agree with these views. Harding soon collected around him a number of enthusiasts who, like Bridson, were to dedicate themselves to the task of getting as many people as possible to speak. It was a task which at first seemed only to involve the craft of journalism but it was to lead fairly swiftly to the creation of a dramatic form of its own. For it was not enough simply to collect a number of speakers; there had to be a theme and a structure and the various voices had to be arranged and co-ordinated. There had also to be a narration. The narration, in bridging the gap between listeners and some relatively unfamiliar group of people, invited some rhetoric and involved on occasions the epic approach. It also lent itself to a heightened prose which bordered on blank verse.

Among the people attracted to Harding's Manchester regime were several who were later to make their impact upon radio and the theatre. There was Francis Dillon, later the winner of many Radio Italia prizes and one of the great instigators of other writers' talents; there was Joan Littlewood, who later applied what she learned in radio to the theatre; there was Ewan MacColl, the singer, and Kenneth Adam, who was to become Director of BBC Television; there was Edgar Lustgarten, who was later to apply his training as a lawyer to countless radio inquiries and accounts of famous trials; and there was Jan Bussell, a drama producer, whose ambition was to become a puppet-master and who later gave Muffin the Mule to television. Bridson recalls the difficulties which they faced, which were both social and technical.

> It seemed to me that since its inception, broadcasting by the BBC had been the exclusive concern of 'us', and listening the lucky privilege of 'them'. That the man in the street should have anything vital to contribute to broadcasting was an idea slow to gain acceptance. That he should actually use broad-casting to express his own opinions in his own unvarnished words, was regarded as almost the end of all good social order. Never once in history had the man in the street been even consulted.[2]

The lack of portable recording equipment at this time conspired to make the access of the man in the street even more difficult. Nearly all speech in the thirties and forties was broadcast live and it had become the accepted custom in Britain to insist that all talks and interviews should be scripted in advance. This applied not only to contributions from the man in the street but to talks by experienced communicators like Bernard Shaw, who was refused the chance of simply coming into the studio to talk off the cuff. Bridson explains the reasoning for this: 'The microphone was regarded as such a potentially dangerous weapon that nobody was allowed to approach it until it was fully known what he intended to do with it.'

It could be argued that the existence of a script ensured that contributors would not over-run their slot in the programmes but there is no doubt that it facilitated the vetting of material and inevitably discouraged contributions from those without some experience in literary communication. It meant that the field of regular broadcasters was limited to politicians, writers, professional actors and public figures, who generally tended to speak in the approved patrician dialect.

The obstacles which Harding and his team faced in Manchester when they sought to get the voices of the people heard were therefore considerable. The BBC insisted that there had to be a script even when a topic was being discussed in a conversational manner. Producer–writers like Bridson and Dillon would go out and talk to potential contributors and take notes of their views. They would then return to the studio and write a script composed from these notes, which their contributors would then have to enact in the studio at the time of the broadcast. Even though they were sympathetic to the views of their contributors, they could on occasion still stand in the way of free and unobstructed expression of opinion. There was in addition no chance for the contributors to alter their views or have second thoughts and there was also the inhibiting environment of the studio which sometimes made the contributors resort to refinements which were not typical of their normal speech. Dillon and Bridson soon resorted to the device of transporting the very large and cumbersome recording equipment to people's houses where they could speak their scripted lines in comfort.

But the BBC's insistence upon scripted documentary programmes was to stimulate an approach to composition which was closer to drama than to journalism. It is interesting that Bridson's account of composing and compiling these early programmes recalls the method of approach employed by Charles Correll and Freeman Gosden when they started broadcasting *Amos n' Andy* in 1928. For a dramatic production a script is, of course, a necessity but, according to Eric Barnouw, Correll and Gosden found that they had to start with the voices and then compile the script. One of them would type out the dialogue while the other paced to and fro, trying out the lines. In order to sustain the sense of immediacy they chose not to rehearse the lines again before broadcasting. Though they were professional actors consciously engaged in the construction of a dramatic dialogue, their manner of composition closely resembles the one which was imposed upon BBC features producers, whose original intention was not the creation of a dramatic form of entertainment.

The format of the phone-in programme, in which listeners may express their dissociated views at random, was then technically impractical. The scripted programmes therefore had to have a stated theme or precise topic for discussion and this naturally involved the device of presentation. With the deliberate intention of widening the scope of such programmes, Bridson hit upon the idea of employing a dramatic character to act as interlocutor. He invented a man called Harry Hopeful, who was played by Frank Nicholls, a clock repairer from Irlam, Lancashire, who was also an amateur actor. Harry Hopeful then played in a series of programmes which had the given story line of a man looking for work in the north of England. This story line allowed Harry Hopeful to travel all over the north of England interviewing people about their various trades and occupations. The programmes were occasionally patronising and sometimes their jovial nature seemed a trifle forced. But they started the process of breaking down the barriers which presumed that northerners were only comic figures of no account. They also suggested a pattern of composition which Bridson and others soon developed.

Dillon, for example, who soon moved to Bristol, which, like Manchester, is a regional capital with a cultural entity of its own, concentrated on dispelling the Mummerset image of rural people but he also turned his radio training to good advantage by writing and adapting several children's stories and fairy tales. Dillon never felt that a documentary feature should merely be a catalogue of information. The characters or contributors in a feature have to convey information in a dramatic form but whereas the visual images evoked in a play must serve the plot, the visual images in a feature must illuminate the theme. He applied some of this thinking to his adaptation of Hans Christian Andersen's *The Nightingale*, which was produced by Val Gielgud in 1935. He then adapted *The Snow Queen*, which has since been repeated on numerous occasions. He next proposed to adapt *The Shirt*, which is about a king who is only happy when he is wearing the shirt of a happy man, but this proposal fell foul of the BBC's fear that it would draw parallels in the minds of the listeners. It was thought to be out of the question to broadcast such a play in 1937 when George VI was about to be crowned.

Meanwhile, Bridson's similar experience in making the voices of the people heard led him to think in terms of a story which would allow the action to move across the country and thus involve these diverse voices. His first feature play of this type was *The March of the '45*, which he wrote in 1933 and which was broadcast in 1936. He chose to write the narrative in verse because he wanted it to be made exciting and what he called 'charged' in a way that prose can never be. He had published poetry in literary magazines but he realised that this kind of poetry would be too esoteric for a mass audience. He realised that his model here ought to be the poetry of Walter Scott. He wrote: 'Rhyming narrative verse has a strongly hypnotic beat to it, comparable in its way to the pounding beat of early jazz: it can hold attention riveted and it can heighten emotional response.'[3]

With this poetic and deliberately rhetorical narrative he not only described the march of the Scottish army in 1745 but set the event against the society and landscape of England in the thirties. The Scots were heard to march south to Derby and north again to their defeat at Culloden as if they were ghosts passing through the present.

> Headstocks line the lanes they followed. The fields
> Are smouldering slag heaps. We have not been idle,
> And staple industries have their yields –
> Wigan her coal and iron. Also the mills –
> In combine, mostly – and the rubber proofers:
> Power and light by pylon from the hills.

Bridson was significantly wary that this popular style might be thought typical of his verse-making. A poet who otherwise contributed to esoteric literary magazines and who knew both Ezra Pound and Hugh MacDiarmid felt that he had to apologise for this lapse into a rougher style. He pleaded the need to appeal to a wider audience but he was already one of those whose ears had been opened to the music of demotic speech which, as Wordsworth had once argued, is an essential literary inspiration. Though radio and its audience was his prime mover his stylistic innovation ought to be compared with MacDiarmid's more conscious and deliberate effort during the same period to assert the merits of Scottish demotic as a fit vehicle for philosophy. In the event he need not have worried about losing literary status. Archibald MacLeish never heard *The March of the '45* but word of it clearly reached him for he acknowledged it as a prototype for *The Fall Of The City*. Louis MacNeice was later to recall its influence upon his own work in the foreword to his play *Christopher Columbus*. Tyrone Guthrie's reaction to it was mixed. In 1938 he wrote to Harding:

> I think as a demonstration of One Of The Things Radio Can Do, the programme had quality. It was a good Sound Picture on a sweeping scale. And I guess as such it broke new ground when it was new. But as a work of art I don't think it is at all important.[4]

Guthrie, who was then working in the theatre and who had just managed after an interval of seven years to get his play *Matrimonial News* performed on radio, may have been suffering a sense of pique. He ought perhaps to have recognised that this work of Bridson's was an effective essay in the style which he had once called symphonic. It was certainly not a history play in the accepted sense but was, as he admits, a good Sound Picture on a sweeping scale. The microphone was here taken out of the studio into the national arena and in place of the social archetypes upon which Guthrie had been forced to depend there were the actual voices of the people. To say that it was not important as a work of art is to slip dangerously into the trap of presuming again that something on radio may be good in its genre but cannot otherwise be given recognition.

Perhaps Guthrie in 1938 was still too close to the event and to

Bridson's other work which heralded the eventual revolution in diction which was to have very important consequences in the theatre. In 1937, Bridson wrote and compiled *Coronation Scot,* a programme which described the passage of an express train from London to Glasgow. His prototype here may well have been Harding's programme for Christmas Day 1932, in which voices from different parts of the world are assembled to report on the state of their countries. On this occasion, the central point in the programme is not the London studio but the train moving through the country. Some newly available portable recording equipment made it possible to record the actual sound of the train entering tunnels, passing through stations and encountering different gradients. But the lasting magic of this moment in radio was the way in which the gradually changing dialects of the railway staff along the route told the listener of the journey. These voices, competent and related to the skills and trades, were true and real and exposed the imperfections of the theatrical imitations of Cockney, Northern and Mummerset.

To hear the people was the important social event but there was another factor in the ingredients of these early features which was to have considerable artistic importance. They required music not merely to provide a scene-setting overture or the isolated song, as in a play, but to give form and pattern throughout the programme. A part of the inspiration here was the use of a musical narrative in films but music was used not only to provide a thematic background but as a foil and comment upon the words. It is apparently thought by some radio feature producers today that they should use music in their programmes because their predecessors did. They therefore take an excerpt from a tape or disc and seem to imagine that by slapping this excerpt on to the opening of the programme they are emulating the earlier style. Feature producers today have the creative disadvantage of being able to rely upon subsequent technical improvements. They can now extract and copy almost any piece of music they require. But in the days when people like Dillon and Bridson made their first programmes, tape-recording had not been perfected and the extraction of excerpts from disc-recordings, without the aid of tape-recorders, was difficult and unreliable. They had, therefore, to employ live orchestras in the studios and quite often had to commission specially written music.

British radio producers were luckily blessed with a plethora of musicians. Thanks to a policy of deliberate patronage of music on the part of the BBC and to the early efforts of the Musicians' Union to establish an agreed balance of live and recorded music on radio, a large number and variety of orchestras were at hand in the studios. The establishing of the feature programme obviously invited their participation and it was to lead to a very rare and profitable association of composers and writers, actors and musicians. The artists of words and music had to work together. Composers like William Walton and Benjamin Britten, whose first BBC commission was to write the music for Bridson's *King Arthur* (1937), were not expected to create their music in isolation without knowledge of or care for the text. The convention of the opera, where the librettist is often the verbal servant of the music, did not apply. The convention of the cinema film, where the music was simply employed as a background effect, was also not applicable. The music sometimes had to become part of the dialogue and the words in performance had likewise to respond musically.

This necessary association of writers and musicians was to lead to a remarkable creative rapport. It was to inform the later work of people like Britten, in whose music the spoken word is always present, and MacNeice, in whose poetry the hint of music is never absent. This kind of artistic cross-reference encompassed all forms of music. It attracted singers like Ewan MacColl, who was first heard by Kenneth Adam busking outside the Manchester Paramount cinema in 1933 and who was then taken on by the BBC both as a singer and as an actor or narrator. MacColl was later to marry Joan Littlewood, who is said to have walked most of the way from London to join the Manchester crowd. She worked on a number of features of which the most memorable is the one devoted to the Durham miners in 1938 and entitled *Coal*. Bridson is undoubtedly right to say that it was no coincidence that Ewan MacColl and Joan Littlewood gathered together a company in Manchester which was later to become the Theatre Workshop company. The experience of matching words to music, the stimulus of listening to the many tongues of English, the discipline of the kind of presentation radio required, were undoubtedly influential in determining the style and approach of Theatre Workshop. It is easy to presume that this theatre company owed its inspiration entirely to the doctrines pronounced by Brecht. But its original catalyst was the radio studio and the community of the radio people in Manchester. The style of a play like *Uranium 235,* which MacColl and Littlewood took on tour in the fifties, was thought by many theatre-goers to be a Brechtian derivative, but even if they had never heard of Brecht, their radio experience would have determined this style and approach. The mixture of song, of direct statement to the audience, of narrated dramatic scenes, is a formula familiar to the radio feature of the thirties.

Intending to make a different point, G. K. Chesterton once wrote a poem which contained the line: 'We are the English, and we have not spoken yet.' In the thirties, from Manchester, some of the English, who had never spoken and were not even supposed to speak, were at last given their tongues. The credit for this development must go to Harding and his associates who argued the logic that a medium of mass communication invited the masses to speak as well as listen. But it should not be thought that their efforts resulted in any grand social revolution. The national audience was pleased to hear new forms of entertainment and the lasting effects of this development were confined to those who worked in the very small radio community. The new voices which got their chance to speak were not very numerous and they were not always able to say exactly what they wanted. The persisting requirement to speak to a script still effectively monitored their contributions. In features which touched upon politically debatable ground, the producers who had managed to get permission to deal with such issues had themselves to monitor their contributors to make sure that they did not cause offence and thus prevent the programme being broadcast.

The BBC could on occasion be unaccountably touchy. Bridson recalls producing a radio version of *The Waste Land* by T. S. Eliot in 1938 when, to the poet's rage, the references to abortion in the poem had to be cut. George Reavy, who was Russian–Irish, sold a number of Russian plays in translation from 1933 onwards but when he offered *Krassin Saves Italia* in 1937 the Foreign Office intervened and prevented the play being broadcast on the grounds that it was pro-Soviet. When the Soviet Union entered the war in 1941, the Foreign Office finally relented but there was still a proviso that the production should not contain the singing of the Red Flag. In 1935 R. F. Delderfield, who was then a journalist working on a weekly newspaper in the west of England, was one of the first of many writers to turn first to the BBC rather than to the theatre as a market for his work. He submitted a play about the war in Abyssinia entitled *Experiment in Futility* which was turned down on the grounds that it was too controversial. He had no better luck with another play in 1937. In 1938 he actually encountered religious censorship when he offered *Spark In Judaea*, which viewed the events of the Crucifixion from the vantage of the Roman soldiers. John Pudney, the poet, who was in charge of scripts, found the play acceptable but he decided to play safe and submitted it to the Religious Department of the BBC, who immediately rejected it on the grounds that its content was 'too realistic'. *Spark In Judaea* was eventually performed successfully in several theatres without causing religious riots but it was banned from the radio.

Some of these examples of censorship were clearly political but some of them were in response to the BBC's continual fear of arousing the anger of some vociferous lobby. Being a state monopoly, the BBC has always been hypersensitive to complaints from letter-writing minorities who can stir up more trouble than their numbers merit. But there was a further paradox in the thirties because the need to provide broad entertainment also meant that the Drama department could not easily find space for experimental work in the way that Columbia Workshop in the USA was able to do. Tyrone Guthrie faced this problem when he offered *Traveller's Joy* in 1939 and it was rejected by Val Gielgud.

On 19 March 1939, Guthrie wrote to Gielgud accusing him of 'making rather an excessive use of the BBC monopoly' in rejecting the play. 'I do suggest that your monopoly places you in a moral obligation not to refuse experiments, even when they are not in accordance with your department's taste, provided that the experiment is a responsible one.'[5] Guthrie claimed that he was one of the first dozen writers who should be allowed and encouraged to experiment even when such experiments might appeal to a minority audience. Gielgud, in his reply, which revealed that five other people had read the play and agreed with his decision, took up this charge of misuse of monopoly.

I don't think that simply because of our monopolistic situation and our absence of box office 'brake' we are entitled to abrogate a considered opinion when a submitted work by however distinguished an author is unlikely to meet the bill as far as popularity is concerned. If I were in the position of the Columbia Workshop – i.e. if I had a regular period each week in which experiments in definitively anti-commercial stuff were worked in as a makeweight to an otherwise entirely commercial output – it would be another matter, but this is not my situation.

The dilemma for Gielgud here was that although British radio offered a far wider range of entertainment than was the case in American radio, it had no cultural ghetto of the kind which Columbia Workshop provided. The Third Programme did not then exist, and although television broadcasting began in Britain in 1937, it was to remain the medium for the minority until the coronation of Queen Elizabeth in 1953. The onus was thus placed upon radio of providing for the mass audience drama which neither offended nor aroused baffled hostility.

But while drama producers worried about causing offence, feature producers enjoyed a much freer rein. Their work was populist. They did not set out to be intellectually experimental. As Francis Dillon once said, 'I don't believe in experiment. I believe in doing it.'[6] He and his colleagues were caught up in the excitement of arguing and compromising with composers and of getting the voices on to the air. In Guthrie's view, this was only proving what radio could do and was not necessarily art, but, whether it is denied the Olympian accolade or not, it undoubtedly provided the foundations for the later development of radio drama. Though it was not the conscious purpose of the feature writer to write a play, the debate contained within the feature argued the creation of a plot. Actors trained in the formal delivery of the theatre learned at last to listen to the speech of that other English which had been so long despised. In the late thirties the comedians still made their jokes about the patrician voices reading the news, and British social class was still sharply determined by the precise use of accent. But in the radio studios, the writers and the poets, the actors and the producers had begun to listen to other voices.

5.
The National Theatre

The circumstances created during the Second World War gave British radio a cultural opportunity which was unique. Like many other radio services in the warring countries, the BBC had to provide propaganda and information. MacNeice, who joined the BBC in 1941, later recalled this particular requirement in his poem *Autumn Sequel*. Paraphrasing the instructions of someone he calls Harrap, who was in fact Archie Harding, he has him say that their job was to feed:

> The tall transmitters with hot news – Dunkirk,
> Tobruk or Singapore, you will have to set
> Traps for your neutral listeners, Yank or Turk,
>
> While your blacked-out compatriots must be met
> Half-way – half-reprimanded and half-flattered,
> Cajoled to half-remember and half-forget. [1]

But the work of poets like MacNeice was not confined to the creation of propaganda. The tall transmitters not only had to supply hot news and exhortation; they had to supply a range of entertainment which had to appeal to intellectual minorities as well as to the mass audience. There was a national mood which looked to the arts for solace and inspiration and, for the five years of the war, British radio was the main medium for this communication and education.

British radio became the national theatre. The fear that theatres might be bombed and the fact that their staffs were directed into more combative employment meant that most of the theatres in the country were closed for the duration of the war. The proud

boast of the Windmill Theatre, London, which offered leg shows
and turns by music-hall comedians – 'We never closed' – makes
the point that there was elsewhere no theatre at all. British television, which had served a small minority audience, was also
closed down, while television in the USA gradually expanded. It
did not supplant radio as the mass medium until 1949 but it
already offered writers and actors an alternative employment in
the USA.

American writers like Jerome Lawrence and Robert E. Lee
were to write propaganda features for radio like their British
contemporaries but radio never enjoyed the cachet common in
Britain. There was a limited outlet for serious work through the
Columbia Workshop for which Lawrence and Lee wrote their
ingenious *Inside a Kid's Head* in 1941, but the American writer was
never able to enjoy that certainty known to the British writer that
his work was speaking to the whole national community. In
Britain the alternative medium of the cinema film did not exist
either and radio therefore became the prime means of communication for dramatic entertainment as well as propaganda.

When the war started, however, this particular need to entertain as well as exhort was not immediately recognised. The fear
that London would face an aerial blitzkrieg, which had caused
the closure of the theatres, also persuaded the BBC's administra-
tors to scrap its existing programmes and normal output and
to despatch most of its staff to the imagined safety of rural
Worcestershire. When the expected bombing did not take place,
public reaction to this curtailment of programmes was predictably hostile and it was left to people like Val Gielgud to argue
the case for an expansion of radio services. In December 1939,
Gielgud outlined his proposed drama policy to the BBC Home
Service Board in the following manner.

It seems to me that few things can be more important during a
war than the preservation of the civilised values for which that
war is being fought. To such preservation the contribution of
Broadcasting can and should be large. On this score, therefore,
I feel we should – as far as is possible – work to re-establish our
pre-war standards of straight drama. Without ignoring in
any way the demand for popular entertainment – Pickwick,
Wodehouse, Wells and Jacobs adaptations, new plays by

authors such as Peach, Giddy and Norman Edwards, and serials (*The Four Feathers, The Three Musketeers,* etc.) – we should find every means to represent the classic drama.[2]

It is a matter of some moment in the history of British drama that Gielgud succeeded in winning this particular argument. He told me many years later that he had been waiting for an opportunity of this nature ever since his appointment as Head of Drama. For many years, there had been a reluctance on the part of the administration to permit the broadcasting of the full classic repertoire because it was feared that some plays of this kind would not appeal to the mass audience. This had meant that the Greek classics, which are eminently suited to radio, and even some of the plays by writers like Ibsen were not thought acceptable. But in 1939 Gielgud was at last able to counter this argument and relate his proposed expansion to the commonly accepted principle that the war against Hitler's Germany represented a struggle to preserve civilised values. He was aided here by the fact that during the war the fairly persistent philistine attitude towards the arts in Britain was relinquished. The hostile prejudice which in the First World War caused Eric Gill, later the sculptor of the façade of Broadcasting House, to be tarred and feathered for daring to be an artist as well as a soldier, was rarely to be found.[3] Seizing the opportunity of a change in the cultural climate, people like Gielgud were at last able to use radio to present the whole range of drama.

This presentation naturally involved some difficulties. Following the removal to Evesham in Worcestershire, the Drama department was established in Manchester, which was mistakenly thought to be safe from aerial attack. This move isolated drama producers from their peace-time connections with the London theatre. But it was fortuitous in one other respect because it brought the drama producers into close daily and working contact with the features producers who had been working under Harding. People whose traditions and training had been largely theatrical began to work alongside those who had been experimenting with more open and random radio forms such as the poetic documentary with its specially composed music. Not everybody believed that the drama producers had much to learn. Harman Grisewood, for example, who began his radio career as an actor and who later became a Director of the BBC, was a great admirer of Gielgud's work and made the following unfavourable comparison in his autobiography, *One Thing At A Time.*

Those who were not rooted in the theatre, Lance Sieveking, E. J. Kingbull and Archie Harding, though they did interesting and sometimes beautiful work, lacked the aesthetic certainty which Gielgud had and which he, and others who were genuine theatre people, Howard Rose or Peter Creswell, could communicate to a cast.[4]

Grisewood does not suggest that people like Bridson or Joan Littlewood or even MacNeice lacked this capacity to communicate with a cast and there can be no doubt that the fusion of Features, under Laurence Gilliam, and Drama, under Val Gielgud, in Manchester was of great importance. Another accident of war which was of benefit was the creation of the Drama Repertory Company. Some drama producers had long felt that productions might be improved if they could call upon actors and actresses who were regularly employed in radio and were therefore better acquainted with its techniques and special requirements. The closing of the theatres and the removal to Manchester destroyed the customary free market for actors upon which the drama producers had depended. It was therefore a necessity to establish this Repertory Company whose members could be on hand to play whatever parts were required in both features and drama.

This company, which has now been in existence for forty years and which has given employment to many actors and actresses of national and international repute, has had its critics, some of whom have regarded it very unjustly as a kind of rest home for failing actors. But this is to ignore the enormous contribution it has made to the art of radio drama and therefore to drama in general. Instead of coming straight from a theatre and having to unlearn the manners of the stage, those who worked for the Repertory Company began to think wholly in radio terms.

Making the actors and actresses a part of the radio community was to have important consequences and there is no doubt, as far as Bridson was concerned, that this company provided an added stimulus.

> As for the Drama Repertory Company, they brought a splendid accession of acting talent to the North, Gladys Young and Laidman Browne, Philip Wade, Ronald Simpson, Ivan Samson and Bryan Powley, Mary O'Farrell and Vivienne Chatterton, Valentine Dyall, Robert Eddison and Edana Romney – these names and a score of others lent new lustre to all our joint productions. The North had never enjoyed such a galaxy of talent before.[5]

But while the north revelled in this talent until the return of the Features and Drama departments to London in 1941, it was radio which gained the greater benefit. The members of the company did not only perform in straight plays; they had speaking parts in features too. They did not merely serve as narrators or as the performers of linking dialogue. Because recording methods were still very primitive it was still the custom to collect material in written form rather in the manner of a newspaper reporter and to have these 'lines' spoken by actors in the studio. This kind of work involved emulating the kind of local and regional speech in which it had first been uttered and this experience was later to contribute to changes in dramatic diction. The absence of tape-recording facilities, which now allow a producer to cut and edit at will, also called upon the actors and actresses to take some part in the editing process themselves. The presence of these people, who could not only act but who were familiar with radio's techniques, was to lead to the creation of a remarkable association of the talents involved in radio production. This manner of working as a group in which actors, engineers, musicians, writers and producers feel they can contribute as equals is still typical of the British radio studio and is rarely found in the theatre or the film studio. In Barbara Coulton's *Louis MacNeice In The BBC*, which provides an invaluable chronicle of the poet's contribution to radio, she remarks upon the fruitful nature of this collaboration and upon how it appealed to MacNeice, who was not an extrovert. 'He enjoyed working with actors, musicians and engineers; he liked the valid nature of the co-operation – it was not a self-indulgent coterie, but a purposeful team.'[6] This agreeable pattern of working as a group could as well allow an experienced radio actor or a studio engineer to offer emendations to the script or suggest improvements to the production without causing offence or hurt pride. It created an atmosphere in which everyone involved felt that they had more than their own part to play in the fashioning of the craft of radio.

There were of necessity not many writers available to radio during the war. There was also, as Mrs Linklater recalls [letter to author] a bias on the part of some literary people against the idea of writing for radio. 'In those days, it was not considered particularly meritorious to write radio plays.' Among those who were already committed to radio and who did not suffer from this curious intellectual snobbery, the pressure of other work made it difficult to find time to write plays. They tended to write features rather than plays, although in the course of time many of these features were so structured that they could well be defined as dramatic entertainment especially written for radio. Francis Dillon, who was the writer, producer and editor of *Country Magazine*, which became one of the most popular weekly programmes during the war, once explained that they simply had not the time to write straight plays.[7] There was a continual demand for propaganda programmes and wartime conditions did not permit the playwright to indulge in detached contemplation in order to present characters in a relaxed perspective. But for those like Dillon and Bridson and MacNeice there was the attractive alternative stimulus of composing radio work which made use of narrative, dialogue and sound effects and of music which was often especially written for the programmes.

It is often thought that the use of specially written music was an excessive luxury which could have been well avoided. But it has to be remembered that the primitive nature of recording techniques at that time did not allow producers to extract excerpts from existing disc-recordings and to employ them as background effect. If a play or a feature seemed to require music, this had to be supplied by an orchestra in the studio where the playing of the music could be adjusted to fit the dramatic needs of the programme. Use of music in this manner soon argued the benefit of having it specially composed and Walton, Britten, Seiber, Hopkins and others contributed specially written music on numerous occasions. The composition of features, which were often disregarded as works of art by those who held to traditional literary fashions, involved and invited considerable artistic ingenuity. Understandably, this kind of work attracted people like MacNeice who could give little time to the writing of straight plays.

The Drama department therefore largely confined its activities to the presentation of more and more plays from the classical repertoire but one interesting dramatic venture followed from Gielgud persuading Eric Linklater to write some dramatic dialogues for radio. The first of these plays was *The Cornerstones*, which he wrote in 1941. It was set, like some of the later dialogues, in the Elysian Fields, where it was therefore possible to gather historical figures from different countries and periods and to allow them to engage in conversation. This conversation was conducted in natural contemporary speech and none of the characters indulged in fustian language. The actors naturally gave their characters accents which accorded with contemporary versions of, for example, Russians speaking English. *The Corner-stones* brought together Abraham Lincoln, Lenin and Confucius, whose conversation is overheard and then interrupted by a young British soldier called Arden who has been killed in North Africa. The propaganda objective of the piece was to identify a common cause among those fighting Hitler's Germany, while acknowledging the obvious philosophical differences in a wry manner. Lenin and Lincoln have to admit the common ground that they were both against slavery, while they find Confucius somewhat predictably remote. Lincoln confesses to Lenin:

I like Confucius but sometimes I feel that if I had been brought up in England, in a cathedral city, I think, and perhaps if I had gone to Winchester and New College, I should be more at home with him. I don't suppose he means it but his manner has, at times, an exasperating superiority that, if it wasn't Chinese, couldn't be anything but English.[8]

Arden breaks in shortly after this, introducing Britain as a country devoted to the notion of fair play. He then voices a fairly popular British self-portrait.

Some countries like to work from a blue-print but we prefer
trial-and-error. The worst of revolution is that it often leads to
counter-revolution, but with trial-and-error you just keep on
trying.

Such sentiments were well received by the majority of
listeners, but Mrs Linklater recalls that a Spitfire pilot who was
invited to listen to the play at their home in the Orkneys was
slightly embarrassed by it. The general reaction was, however,
very good and Gielgud wanted Linklater to write some more
plays. The writer was then a Captain in the Royal Engineers so
Gielgud tried to get him extra leave. The BBC has a fairly noble
record as a constructive patron but Gielgud's effort on Linklater's
behalf was surely exceptional. On 24 April 1942 he wrote to the
War Office asking that he be given special leave to write radio
plays. *Of The Cornerstones*, he wrote:

The effect of this play as a reinforcement of public morale and
an incentive to victory was very marked. Captain Linklater has
informed us that he has in mind two or more plays specifically
designed for the strengthening of the will-to-victory, which at
the present time is so urgently needed.[9]

The War Office replied very properly that no such leave could be
given but on 12 May 1942 Linklater was posted to the Directorate
of Public Relations with the duty of Propaganda and Publicity
Literature and a brief to write radio plays, which he was allowed
to work at from his home in the Orkneys. By 13 June 1942 he had
finished *The Raft* and he later wrote *Socrates Asks Why*, *The Great
Ship* and *Rabelais Replies*, all of which followed the pattern he had
established in *The Cornerstones*.

Historical figures were brought together in a manner which
echoed the capacity of news bulletins to bring voices together
from different parts of the world. But they spoke to each other in
the style of contemporary conversation and, though the sentiments they expressed might now seem out of place, the example
of these dialogues was not lost upon later writers for radio and
the theatre. Linklater did not write for radio after the war and his
contribution was an exception to the general rule which during

the war determined that most of the interesting work, from both a technical and artistic point of view, emanated from the Features department, headed by Laurence Gilliam. Gilliam, who was also a producer, must be rated as one of the great catalysts. He was a great encouragement to other people's talent and was always ready to assist experiment. The format which was required in straightforward propaganda features, which involved narration, actuality recordings, dialogue inserts and music which was sometimes on records and sometimes specially commissioned, served as a model of instruction which producers like MacNeice, Bridson and Dillon then applied to the creation of dramatic entertainments. Some of these works would now be described as radio plays but their creators tended always to refer to them as features, a term which can on occasion lead to some confusion. In the introduction to *Christopher Columbus* (broadcast 2 October 1942), MacNeice wrote:

> The radio feature is a dramatised presentation of actuality but its author should be much more of a rapporteur or a cameraman; he must select his actuality material with great discrimination and then keep control of it so that it subserves a single dramatic effect. [10]

This observation could well apply to many of the works which MacNeice wrote for the BBC but it hardly applies to *Christopher Columbus*, which was a play for radio, although the exercise of discrimination and control of the material involved in a radio work is certainly present.

What is unfortunate is that the intellectual bias against radio naturally encouraged some ignorance of its methods and of the qualities of discrimination and control which it requires. There is a fairly lively folklore concerning the years of the Features department's heyday both during and after the war which presupposes that people like MacNeice and composers like Benjamin Britten or William Walton, who wrote the music for *Christopher Columbus*, just knocked the whole thing together while carousing in some pub or club close to Broadcasting House. But such myths may be dispelled by revealing the painstaking instructions which someone like MacNeice provided his composers. A producer had not only to concern himself with careful selection of the actuality material; he had also to provide very precise instructions to the composers.

In 1947, when he had been working in radio for six years, MacNeice chose to adapt the Icelandic story of *Grettir The Strong* and Matyas Seiber was asked to write the music for it. MacNeice did not presume that the music would only be an embellishment; he clearly required it to become an integral part of the drama. We may gain some appreciation of his meticulous approach from this list of musical cues which he supplied to Seiber.

2. Sea-faring music taking Grettir away from Iceland. Cue in from his mother, 'May God bring you safe to Norway' and fade behind sailors' dialect beginning 'Leak? Half a dozen leaks.' This is followed by about a minute's dialogue, after which the sea music starts again.

2A. About 20 seconds – N.B. the sea is steadily getting rougher; over this we have first female giggles, and then grunts and groans from the crew. To fade behind first line of following dialogue from Grettir, 'Hallo, fellows. What are you up to, baling?'

3. More dialogue for about a minute after which baling music fades in No. 3. N.B. This is a continuous number, consisting of (a) about 15–20 seconds intro. to establish the baling process, and the stepping up of same, (b) in background to half a dozen lines of dialogue, ending, '4 men take over on deck', (c) Music alone stepping up again (anything from ten seconds upwards, just as long in fact as it takes you to make your point), (d) In background to short speech by Captain (C.4 lines) ending, 'You eight take over at the buckets', (e) Music along to close, getting faster and faster and more hectic. The close represents that the ship is completely baled out.

4. Introduction to cairn scene. Cue from Grettir preparing to descend by a rope: 'Here goes'. About 20 seconds. Over which Grettir, apart from grunts, will say to himself, 'Gently . . . gently . . . there!' The 'there' should synchronise with the close of the music. He has landed on the floor of the chamber.[11]

This is only a small quotation from MacNeice's notes to Seiber

which clearly leave very little to chance. MacNeice obviously did
not believe that his task was ended when he had written the
dialogue. On occasion, he allows the composer some latitude, as,
for example, when he writes in Cue 3(c) that the music should be
'anything from ten seconds upwards, just as long in fact as it
takes you to make your point.' But in Cue 4, it is clear that
MacNeice is hearing in advance of the composition and of the
eventual performance, the complete integration of the music
with the grunts as well as the voice of the actor.

When he wrote *Christopher Columbus*, he sent a somewhat
similar outline to William Walton. There was a need in this piece
for one dominant theme of the kind which is required in a cinema
film. But there are also sea shanties and music was required to
indicate changes of scene. When the *Te Deum* is sung to celebrate
Columbus's arrival in the New World, it is contrasted with music
suggestive of the Caribbean. There is no doubt that features like
this were considerably enhanced by the music which was
specially written for them. But the critical tendency to under-
estimate the quality of work written for this form of radio drama
has given rise to the conclusion that the creative benefit flowed
only from the composers and that they gained little from this
traffic in radio.

There can surely be no doubt that composers learned a great
deal from this experience which then informed their later work
for concert or opera. It was not enough to compose the kind of
music required in a cinema film; the music often had to partici-
pate in the dramatic action. It was rarely employed, in the
manner of an opera, to give unwanted rhythms to speeches
indicating changes of mood or scene. It often had to make a choric
point or serve as a witty adjunct to the sound effects, the grunts
and the voices. It required not only MacNeice's discrimination
and control but some great precision.

Christopher Columbus was not only significant because Walton
wrote the music for it. It was the first of MacNeice's dramatic
works for radio which was devoted to the theme of the solitary
epic hero in pursuit of a quest. It was a theme which he was to
employ on a number of subsequent occasions. MacNeice wrote
that he intended to portray Columbus 'as an egoist, uncom-
promising and difficult in his dealings with other people'. The
play begins when he is trying to persuade everyone that his

voyage is worth undertaking at all. There is no narrator leading the listener through the story but MacNeice employed the two voices of Doubt and Faith to argue Columbus's case and to summarise the arguments of those who are either for or against this headstrong man. It might be thought that this celebration of the 450th anniversary of the discovery of the New World was a piece of wartime escapism but MacNeice's notion of the playwright as a teller of parables has some relevance here. There is by implication the acknowledgement of America and the hero is, after all, a man who is intent upon success and who achieves his victory despite all the odds and the doubts. This oblique reference to matters of current concern may be thought by some to be too remote. A poet like Hugh MacDiarmid was fond of castigating MacNeice and his fellow poets, Auden and Spender, for failing to write:

> A poetry that can put all its chips on the table
> And back it to the limit.

It can well be said that, in MacDiarmid's terms, these poets sometimes appeared to pull their punches. It can also be argued that MacNeice's somewhat withdrawn nature led him to favour the understatement rather than the barrage. But it may well be the case that he was led into this style of understatement by the requirements of radio. In *The Story Of My Death* (8 October 1943; repeated 1952) the target is Italian Fascism but the feature carefully avoids overt preaching. It tells the story of the Italian poet, Lauro de Bosis, who in 1931 flew over Mussolini's Rome dropping leaflets and then crashed. As the poet flies over the city he engages in soliloquy. It is perhaps typical of MacNeice that he later made no comment on the play's political implications confining himself to the comment that it presented him with some interesting technical problems. His interest in radio's technique was enormous and it should be appreciated more than it is that this interest was informed by his approach to the craft of poetry. Radio offered a new means of poetic expression. A feature could be shaped like a poem and its verbal contents ordered and arranged with as much discipline and control as can be found in a poem.

While many of his fellow poets spurned radio, he enjoyed

trying to solve the problems of diction which it presented. In the appendix to *Christopher Columbus* he wrote:

> In our twentieth century at any rate dramatic verse – whether for stage or the air – must be flexible enough to fit a wide diversity of characters, to move from the heights to the flats without an obvious change of technique such as Shakespeare's breaks into prose; a stage play that shows this flexibility is Mr Eliot's *Family Reunion*. Radio especially should avoid a sustained metronomic beat which would march into the listener's parlour like a platoon of guardsmen.[12]

It is interesting that when Bridson wrote his *March Of The '45*, he actually opted for the sustained metronomic beat. He says that he sought out a style which would be rousing and declamatory and that he chose the poetry of Walter Scott as his model.

Bridson, on this occasion, actually wanted the platoon of guardsmen to march into the listeners' parlours but during the years which had passed since the performance of this pioneer work, radio producers had learned that better results could often be achieved by understatement.

It was inevitable that MacNeice and his colleagues were sometimes expected and encouraged to resort to a style which they knew to be inappropriate. Barbara Coulton describes such a conflict of intentions when Laurence Gilliam invited MacNeice to write a feature to celebrate the D-Day landing in June 1944. She says that Gilliam preferred a style which tended to be rhetorical.[13] It might be fairer to say that in his enthusiasm as a progenitor he sometimes overstepped the mark. Obviously he felt that the D-Day landing required something which was in the spirit of the speech at Harfleur in Shakespeare's *Henry V*. But MacNeice responded with a script which was much more low key and contemplative, in which a soldier voiced the kinds of thoughts which people normally keep to themselves. It did not shout or beat the drum and Gilliam must have been a little disappointed that his poet had declined to blow the trumpet of war. The style of the piece was not unlike that which MacNeice employed in *He Had A Date*, which was broadcast later the same month (June 1944). This play, which MacNeice would have called a feature, was a commemoration of Graham Shepard, a very old friend who died on an Atlantic convoy. It features a character called Tom Varney who is on watch on board a naval ship in the Atlantic. This setting allows Varney to recall incidents in his past life, starting with childhood and moving on to student days at Oxford, working for a provincial newspaper and eventually joining the navy at the outbreak of war. Various events like the General Strike of 1926, the Spanish Civil War and Munich impinge upon his story, which also contains references to his unhappy marriage to a Scots girl and his meeting, when he has joined the navy, with a girl he had known at Oxford.

There is nothing strident about this story. Summarised in this fashion it may even appear rather pedestrian, but the quiet manner in which it was told made it a moving experience for many people who might have found a more explicit tale slightly embarrassing.

MacNeice knew very well that there were at this stage in the war too many things that were close to tears. During a period when the pressure for propaganda had often insisted upon bombast and the blowing of ritual trumpets, he knew that it was often better to say only just enough rather than too much and his experience as a radio technician confirmed this view. He had learned to be chary of using excessive sound effects and he applied the same doctrine of economy to his choice of words. He would have agreed with the observation of his fellow poet, W. R. Rodgers, who once said that the writer's first task lies in knowing how best to use the small words. It is fortunate that a poet of MacNeice's stature chose to work in radio during this period. The establishment of the style and structure of the radio feature, which often had to serve the commands of government rather than the aspirations of the individual writer, nevertheless demanded the presence of writers who looked upon their task as a disciplined craft. There was the need to find a form of diction which not only appealed to a poet's ear but which was in accord with the rhythms and patterns of ordinary speech. There was also the requirement to control and yet take full advantage of specially written music. In the company of composers like Britten and Walton, MacNeice had to become not merely a poet writing a radio script. He had to compose the script with a musical composer's ear as well. His wartime service was to prepare him to write some of the greatest works for radio which have been

written in English and his example was later to inspire many
other writers.

6.
The Arrival of the Poets

It might be supposed that when the war ended in 1945 and the traditional markets in the theatre and in publishing were revived in Britain, the attraction of radio as a market for literary and dramatic talents was diminished. But during the war, radio had become a great cultural force and the focus of attention of any thinking man or woman. It had not merely become the national theatre, offering under Gielgud's direction a repertoire which included plays not commonly performed even in university theatres. Because the rationing of newsprint limited the space devoted to feature articles in newspapers, radio's features directed by Gilliam had become the principal means of discussing a wide variety of social and cultural matters of interest. Their use of music specially composed for the occasion made Portland Place the cultural centre for composers and musicians as well as poets, dramatists and writers of all kinds. Many returning ex-servicemen with similar interests therefore looked first to radio for employment and an outlet for their talent. There was little opportunity for such people in films; television, which was revived in 1946, was still a limited market.

Radio therefore attracted a large number of talented people with diverse experience and knowledge who were to act as the agents and catalysts of a welter of literary and dramatic talents in the following twenty years. This mass medium was regarded as intellectually and aesthetically attractive by people who in other countries would only have found employment in universities. The poet Terence Tiller and Howard Newby, who was later to become both a novelist and head of the Third Programme, joined the BBC at this time. So also did Joe Burroughs and R. D. Smith, who both hailed from Birmingham where R. D. Smith had met

MacNeice before the war. Smith already had some radio experience; in 1945 he was in charge of English programmes for the Palestine Broadcasting Service in Jerusalem. But this kind of apprenticeship was rare. Rene Cutforth, for example, who was to become a distinguished radio reporter and feature writer, had no previous experience.

Returning from a German prisoner-of-war camp, where he had acquired a knowledge of Russian from his fellow prisoners, he had written occasional newspaper articles before the war. He therefore looked for work as a reporter but was sensibly advised that he might find better scope for his talent in radio. Others who were drawn into the coterie of radio at this time were the Ulster poet, W. R. Rodgers and Eric Ewens, who in 1945 was a lecturer in English at King's College, London. They entered radio at a time when its activities, far from being curtailed, were actually expanding. Gilliam now took the opportunity of sending many of his features producers abroad to make documentary reports. Bridson, for example, who was now his deputy, reported from Norway, Czechoslovakia and Yugoslavia, while MacNeice was later to make a feature in Rome. This kind of reportage still depended to a great extent on the literary quality of the narrative for its success. Tape-recording, which later allowed the form of narration which merely cued the inserts, was not yet available and the cumbersome disc-recording apparatus could on occasion inhibit contributors and sometimes prevent them speaking at all. Michael Barsley, who was later to establish the BBC TV programme *Panorama*, compiled a series at this time which was devoted to the revival of peace-time activities like circuses and garden fêtes. He recalls trying to interview Billy Smart, the circus king, at Ealing and being told to remove that so-and-so frying-pan – the microphone – from the circus man's face. Smart refused to be recorded. This kind of refusal was not frequent but difficulties with recordings encouraged the alternative of compiling features which made use of quotations which could be spoken by actors in a studio. This alternative necessarily required writers and producers of some learning and scholarship and it is not therefore surprising that people like Ewens, Rodgers and Tiller found this radio form attractive.

At the centre of all this activity were people like Dillon and MacNeice. Having performed his wartime service, MacNeice could possibly have left the BBC at this time. In his poem *Autumn Sequel* he recalls this moment, making his decision to stay in radio sound somewhat typically diffident. He wrote:

> . . . 'if you so desire,'
> My employers said, 'this office will now return
> To a peacetime footing where we might require
> Your further service,' I could not discern
> Much choice; it might be better to give
> Such service, better to bury than to burn.[1]

This suggestion that his decision to stay on was made with some reluctance does not reveal the energy and enthusiasm he was devoting to radio at this time. He was already at work on his masterpiece, *The Dark Tower* (broadcast 1946), and was engaged in coaching his fellow poet, W. R. Rodgers, in the mysteries of radio. Rodgers, who was then a clergyman in Ireland, had written a feature about Armagh, entitled *City Set On A Hill*, which MacNeice produced and for which he commissioned William Alwyn to compose the music. It was this collaboration which was to lead to Rodgers leaving Ireland and joining the BBC in London, where he shared an office with MacNeice for a time. Rodgers was to become a member of that radio coterie which, when it was not working in offices or studios, tended to foregather in pubs near Broadcasting House like The George and The Stag. For twenty years after the war The George became not merely the green room for writers, actors and technicians; it became the British equivalent of Les Deux Magots in Paris and there can be very few writers and composers who never stood at its bars. Some writers and critics who held to the mandarin view that working for radio could not have any aesthetic importance because it served a mass audience naturally disliked its atmosphere. They could not stomach the radio people's small talk which, on MacNeice's part, was usually diverted to his lifelong interest in Rugby football. Possibly because they felt excluded, they cultivated the myth that most of the radio coterie were perpetually drunk. A very respected critic recently reiterated this myth when in 1980 he reviewed Barbara Coulton's book on MacNeice, saying that he had found the poet aloof and rude and attributed this attitude to drink. MacNeice certainly liked a drink but he was also a shy man and in conversation preferred the ambiguous parable to direct and specific discussions of poetic theory and practice. Those who expected or demanded such discussions while the poet was relaxing from the concentration the craft of radio requires naturally got short shrift from MacNeice, as they did also from his frequent companion, Dylan Thomas. When Thomas was living near Oxford immediately after the war, he was frequently to be seen in the vicinity of Broadcasting House, where he served a radio apprenticeship which was later to inform his approach to the writing of his play *Under Milk Wood*.

Thomas's first connection with radio had been in 1937 when he came to London in the company of Robert Pocock, who later became a radio producer. He broadcast some of his poems and in 1940 wrote some scripts for the BBC's Latin American service, but his real apprenticeship to radio began when he started acting in plays and features written by his friends. Dillon was the first to use him in this way when he gave him a part in one of his *Civilians' War* series (No 19) in 1941. Douglas Cleverdon, who insists that Thomas's approach to acting was studious and painstaking, then hired him in 1942 to play the part of Private Dai Evans in his adaptation of David Jones's book *In Parenthesis*. This adaptation by Cleverdon was to have been broadcast on 11 November 1942, but was cancelled to make way for a speech by Churchill. Thomas later played the same part in the 1946 production. In 1946 he acted in a number of plays and features. He played in MacNeice's *The Heartless Giant*, which was a dramatisation of a Norwegian folk tale, in Dillon's production of *Private Popski's Army* and in MacNeice's *Trimalchio's Feast*, and he also played the lead part in MacNeice's *Aristophanes*. He also took part in a feature on Thomas Bewick by John Arlott and in an Overseas Service feature by Reggie Smith, and he read Milton's lines in Cleverdon's productions of *Comus* and *Paradise Lost*. In 1947 the BBC's Belfast studios witnessed a rare gathering of poetic talent when Thomas played the Narrator in Rodgers's *The Hare*, which was produced by MacNeice.

There can be no doubt that this experience as a radio actor had some influence upon his writing. With the experience of working as a radio actor still fresh in his mind, Thomas proposed a play to Philip Burton at BBC Cardiff in 1947 which he then called *The Village Of The Mad*.

It was this proposal which several years later was to be resolved in the play now known as *Under Milk Wood*. This play has been staged with some success and Thomas first performed it in the form of readings in the USA while on poetry-reading tours. But it is essentially a work for radio and its format owes much to the advice and assistance given by Douglas Cleverdon, who eventually produced it on radio shortly after Thomas's untimely death in 1953. In the years when Thomas was writing it, he confessed to Cleverdon that the idea lacked dramatic structure and he struggled for some time to impose a plot on it. Cleverdon advised him to forget about the plot and to construct it along the lines of a radio feature, in which the sequence of events simply moved from morning to night. The style of diction which Thomas employed in this play is rhetorical and formal and in this respect it differs from the more conversational style employed by others like Beckett and Pinter, who were responding to the evidence of speech styles which radio offered to them. But the play's structure and its concept of a microphone hanging in mid-air above the village of Llaregyb was undoubtedly suggested to the poet by his experience of radio acting and by his association with the radio coterie.

But this is to anticipate later events. In the immediate post-war period, there was another development of radio policy in Britain which was to have considerable cultural and artistic importance. Sir William Haley, who was then Director General of the BBC, felt that the range of entertainment offered by the two main wavelengths, the Home Service and the Light Programme, was inadequate and that there needed to be another wavelength which would be devoted to the broadcasting of serious music and drama. He therefore established the Third Programme in 1946. It may now seem strange but there were many opponents to the establishment of this programme. It was feared that its necessary appeal to a minority audience would mean that works which might otherwise have been broadcast on the Home Service would fail to reach the mass audience. During the war, the Home Service had been responsible for widening the tastes and interest of the mass audience.

Bridson recalls that Sir Basil Nicholls, who was then Director of Programmes, was against the idea.

Sir Basil Nicholls was not alone in his opposition to the creation of the Third Programme. Nor was Lord Reith the only one outside the BBC who was critical of it when it came. Many others were opposed to it in principle also, some of them with far more experience in planning radio than Sir William Haley, whose love child the Third Programme was. The verb 'to broadcast' means to disseminate widely; and it seemed to many people that to confine the best in radio to one exclusive wavelength could only result in disseminating it most narrowly.[2]

The idea of creating a kind of intellectual ghetto naturally did not appeal to people like Bridson who had been dedicated for so long to the policy of widening the range of entertainment offered to the mass audience on the Home Service. But in retrospect he had to conclude that the Third in its heyday, when its hours were not so limited and it was not so severely restricted to music as it is today, did bring some indisputable benefits. He wrote:

> It soon established itself as the pace-maker and trend-setter of radio. Without its encouragement, the work of the avant garde in literature and music would have been far slower to find a national audience. The fact that their radio audience was small certainly did no disservice to such work; a larger audience would have greeted it only with incomprehension and derision. The best audience anywhere for experimental work has always been small and discriminating. Played to such an audience, experimental work can be fairly judged – it can get itself talked about until it is generally accepted.[3]

It would be inaccurate to assume that Bridson is here describing developments which took place immediately the Third Programme was established. It did not become the arena for avant-garde experiment in its early years. There was a tendency on the part of the Drama department to concentrate on the production of more plays from the classic repertoire which could now find a convenient outlet on the Third Programme.

In this early post-war period, the more interesting innovations which were to influence the approach of other writers tended to emanate from those who were writing and producing features rather than plays. They did not set out to be experimental in a deliberately avant-garde manner; they were responding to the challenge of radio and finding ways of making dramatic points. They did not set out to shock or to break down traditional prejudices; they were much more interested in making radio work. In 1946, for example, the two works which probably made the greatest impact on young listeners who were later to become writers for radio and the stage were not plays in the strict sense. They were MacNeice's *The Dark Tower* and Cleverdon's adaptation of David Jones's *In Parenthesis.* Bernard Kops, when he was a teenager haunting the cafés of Soho, actually founded a group known as 'The Dark Tower Society' and there is no doubt that the production and numerous repeats of *In Parenthesis* had similar effects on the minds of many other young writers.[4]

Cleverdon's long love affair with this book began in 1938 when it won the Hawthornden Prize and he was running a bookshop in Bristol. In 1939 he joined the production staff of *Children's Hour* in Bristol and came under the tutelage of Francis Dillon who was then producing features there. He originally planned to produce *In Parenthesis* on 11 November 1939, but the curtailment of programmes at this time prevented its production. The 1942 production was also cancelled for reasons already given and it was almost eight years before he was able to realise his ambition of presenting it on radio. It is interesting that Jones, according to Cleverdon, did not entirely share this ambition. He did not like the idea of presenting the work in a dramatic form with sound effects and the use of several voices. He would have preferred to have read the whole work aloud himself. He was originally a painter and sculptor and his approach to the composition of literature was in accord with the older and then outmoded practice of writing to be heard as well as to be seen on the page. If radio had not been invented and Cleverdon had not conceived the embellishment of the work in a radio form, Jones would no doubt have resorted to the practice of public solo readings of it. Jones was not a dramatist and he did not compose his work with the intention of it being performed by different voices.

Despite his understandable reservations it should, however, be no surprise that a literary work composed in the manner traditional in both Wales and Ireland, in which the writers presume that their words can also be heard, should be so successful on radio. But apart from its suitability for the medium, the subject also had its appeal. Even in 1946, when another world war had been fought, the tragedy and horrors of the First World War still brooded in the imagination and memories of the British public. Jones himself, who had served in that war, began to write his book in 1929, according to Harman Grisewood, who was one of his oldest friends. Like many others, he had the need to lay the ghost of this terrible experience but he also sought to relate his story to the early Celtic experiences and legends, making his Welsh soldiers in the trenches at one with those who had fought far more ancient battles. He brings to life not only the horrors of trench warfare but goes into meticulous detail, as in this description of an artillery barrage:

> Out of the vortex, rifling the air as it came – bright, brass-shod Pandoran; with all-filling screaming the howling crescendoes up-piling snapt. Behind 'E' battery, fifty yards down the road, a great many mangolds up-rooted, pulped, congealed with chemical earth, spattered and made slippery the rigid boards leading to the emplacement. The sap of vegetables slobbered the spotless breech-block of No. 3 gun.

And against this sharply observed kind of photograph of the events of that war, Jones also has his Welshmen and his Londoners brooding on the Albion for which their forefathers fought against the Roman legions. And there are other battles which are recalled, as when Private Dai Evans, who was played by Dylan Thomas, says: 'My fathers were with the Black Prince of Wales at the passion of the blind Bohemian king. They served in these fields.'

It might be thought that such allusions are remote and unreal and the by-product of a romantic approach on the part of a historically-minded artist. The idea of associating Welsh soldiers of 1915 with their ancestors who fought with the Black Prince in the fourteenth century or with their even earlier forebears who fought the Romans in Britain may seem too fanciful. But when the work was broadcast there were few complaints on this score. Harman Grisewood offers the credible explanation that in times of war people tend to look far back into history and beyond, into legend and myth, for their inspiration and their sense of purpose and identity. In a talk on the Welsh Home Service in 1966, which was devoted to an appreciation of Jones's work, he made this point in the following way.

> The Armada and Waterloo have less relevance to our own time than the impact of the Roman *imperium* upon Celtic Britain. The assimilation of *Romanitas* when the legions left is nearer to the front page of the daily newspaper than the Long Parliament or the reign of William and Mary.

Jones nodded in the direction of the much earlier British inheritance, drawing attention to the fact that while many villages and towns in England have Saxon names, the hills and the rivers still bear their ancient Celtic names. His London, which he left to fight in the trenches, is also the place containing the White Hill where the skull of Bran the Blessed is said to lie buried. This splicing of ancient myth with the horrid reality of twentieth-century war probably appealed, for the reasons which Grisewood gives, but there was another factor which assisted. The radio does not only allow the writer to transport the listener's imagination to remote places and distant times. It has the capacity to tell more than one story at the same time. It may be used to tell a story from the remote past while hinting at an analogy with the present. If it is credible to accept dramatisation of characters in a wartime trench, it is also credible to accept the imaginings of these characters. This is the more possible in radio than in the theatre or on television where the actors are seen and are reminders always of the present.

In most radio drama productions of this particular period this sense of stage presence was still noticeable. When the classic repertoire was presented, there was relatively little attempt to adjust or adapt such plays to radio. But the feature writers and producers who were principally interested in getting their message across made as much use of radio as they could. During the war, they had developed the technique of telling more than one version of the same story at the same time. Sometimes they had used allegory or, as MacNeice preferred, the artifice of the parable. Even the duty of creating deliberate propaganda had also encouraged a style which had to avoid stating the banal and the obvious but which yet conveyed its purpose. British listeners had thus become accustomed to a style which might or might not

carry two messages at once. It is ironic, but in all probability
Cleverdon's adaptation of *In Parenthesis* would have met with
incomprehension and derision if it had been broadcast in 1939
when the listeners had not become as sophisticated as the wartime features had made them.

The diction of *In Parenthesis* closely approaches Welsh oratory
and the heightened language of ancient epic and it could not be
said that Jones's language inspired later dramatists. Its poetic
style is very distant from the careful colloquialism of MacNeice's
poetry and his radio work, but it has to be remembered that
though he wrote for the listening reader he was not a dramatist.
His example is that of a poet who spoke. And although
Cleverdon's adaptation is ingenious he would be among the first
to say that it comes nowhere near the dramatic ingenuity of
MacNeice's *The Dark Tower*. Donald McWhinnie has said of this
work that it represents a textbook of radio technique. It utilised
most of the devices which MacNeice had learned so pain-
stakingly during his wartime radio service. Benjamin Britten
wrote the music for it which, thanks to Britten's previous close
experience of working in radio, is not a mere embellishment
but plays a part in the dramatic action. Though the work was
produced by MacNeice under the aegis of the Drama department, its structure has more in common with the features techniques prevailing at this time. It is, like many of MacNeice's other
works, the story of a quest in which the central figure moves
through from scene to scene in the manner of a radio reporter
examining a particular social problem or political issue. It does
not set out the equation of a dramatic problem to be solved.

The origin of MacNeice's inspiration was Browning's line,
'Childe Roland to the dark tower came.' His Roland comes from a
family whose men have always fought against evil, and when his
brother Gavin dies, Roland is the only one left to carry on the
fight. His mother urges him to do his duty and his Tutor instructs
him, but he is not cut out to be a hero and does not really want to
take on the quest for the dark tower. Casual and almost flippant,
he would prefer to dally with his lover, Sylvie, who wants him to
lead the quiet suburban life. But the Tutor goads him and the
Sergeant schools him in military discipline and his mother gives
him a ring with a blood-red stone which will only lose its colour if
ᶠails in his resolve. Moving as in a dream or on a journey,

Roland encounters other symbols of his time. There is The Dragon, a symbol of Fascism, who tells how he became an informer and thus sent countless people to their deaths. There is an alcoholic intellectual, who represents MacNeice's satirical view of some of his contemporaries. Then he is tempted like Ulysses by Neaera and also by Sylvie, who takes him to a haunted chapel where he hears the voices of his father and his brothers. Then he is mocked by a parrot and a raven; and, not really wishing to be a hero, he is glad when the blood-red stone loses its colour. He then realises that he has the choice to desert this quest but, at this moment, the mountains appear and the trumpets sound to reveal the vision of the dark tower. The work thus ends with the implication that this reluctant hero must face his destiny.

It is difficult to resist the observation that the figure of Roland is to a certain extent autobiographical. A democrat and a socialist, MacNeice knew where the evils lay but he was a quiet man who still regretted the necessary violence which had to be employed to defeat these evils. Roland's reluctance does not commend itself to those who did not share the author's civilised reservations but even those who were prepared to argue against the philosophy contained in *The Dark Tower* were ready to acclaim its artistry and ingenuity. Even those who had never worked in radio and who had previously despised it as a medium for dramatic work of any intellectual merit now had to change their minds.

Barbara Coulton records the instant reaction of Henry Reed, who was later to write many radio plays and who had previously regarded radio only as a means of hearing good music. He wrote to congratulate MacNeice and there can be no doubt that *The Dark Tower* made him think more seriously about the opportunities which radio offered.[5] For intelligent listeners like Reed it demonstrated new ways of dealing with matters of philosophical concern but it also made an impression upon MacNeice's radio colleagues. Cleverdon felt that, technically, it demonstrated complete mastery of the radio form. McWhinnie, who was later to apply the techniques pioneered in features productions to the production of radio plays, was full of admiration for its use of brilliantly simple transitions of scene. One of his examples is the following, in which Roland's movement is depicted and implied without any overt scene setting or effects and without a word for Roland.

TUTOR: Go!
                  Yes, Roland, my son. Go quickly.
                  (WE CROSS TO)
SYLVIE: But why must you go so quickly?

Devices like this are the creation of an accomplished poet who was also a radio craftsman. MacNeice was not alone among his producer colleagues in the features studios in seeking this kind of economy. Under the enthusiastic direction of Gilliam, who wrote in the BBC Year Book for 1946 that 'radio must initiate or die, publish or be damned', they were encouraged to seek new forms and to commission new writers. In 1946, while the Drama department concentrated largely upon radio adaptations of classic plays and novels, people like John Betjeman, Elizabeth Bowen, George Orwell, John and Rosamund Lehmann, Viola Meynell, Geoffrey Grigson and Laurie Lee were persuaded to write features. At the same time, Reyner Heppenstall initiated a series called *Imaginary Conversations*, a form which was inspired by Linklater's wartime dialogues like *Cornerstones*. This form proved extremely attractive to writers who were not dramatists and within a year several writers who were new to radio made some interesting contributions.

C. V. Wedgwood, for example, wrote *Dr Evelyn At Windsor Castle*, which was a conversation between Evelyn and Prince Rupert; Herbert Read wrote *Aristotle's Mother* (Aristotle talking to Apelles and Protagenes); Rose Macaulay wrote *Champion of Freedom* (Milton talking to two Scottish divines); Sean O'Faolain wrote *The Train To Banbury* (J. H. Newman talking to Charles Kingsley); G. W. Stonier wrote *Ophelia*, in which Ophelia talks to Hamlet; Michael Innes wrote *Strange Intelligence*, involving Dr Johnson, Boswell and Lord Monoboddo; V. S. Pritchett wrote *The Gambler*, depicting Dostoevsky and Turgenev. Cleverdon has written an interesting summary of these works.

These were all dramatised to some degree, and localised, with subsidiary characters and crowd effects as required; occasionally there was a narrator. Where the dialogues were undramatic in themselves, the actors had to attune themselves to a conversational tone. In some cases the dialogues were expanded from short entries in a journal such as Evelyn's *Diary* or, as in the case of *The Train To Banbury*, were largely based on published correspondence. Others like *The Gambler* were practically radio plays. *Ophelia*, commissioned for a series of programmes celebrating Shakespeare's birthday, was brilliantly conceived as a possible scene clarifying the reasons for Ophelia's madness. The series admirably illustrated the fluidity of this radio genre. As there was no fixed convention (as there used to be, for example, with the three-act stage play), the writer could determine the form that suited his style and his material.[6]

Much of this work was written for the Third Programme and the fact that it was written by scholars, novelists and biographers and not dramatists is significant. People like V. S. Pritchett, G. W. Stonier and Sean O'Faolain did not set out to write these dialogues with any preconceived dramatic notions. Their first interest was to display the thinking and emotions of their chosen subjects and to present them through the living voice. They were often presenting historical figures that few dramatists of that time would have considered fit subjects for plays.

They did not pretend to be playwrights and they often left the presentation and dramatisation in the hands of the producers, who made sure, for example, that actors delivered what Cleverdon calls 'the undramatic' in a 'conversational tone'. The relationship between these writers and their producers was very similar to the one which Francis Watson has described when he first wrote for radio in 1937. He had written his first novel and Francis Dillon had asked him to write something for radio.

To me it seemed that, like writing for the stage, it required a technique that I had not yet studied. 'Fade in, Fade out,' he (Dillon) replied. 'That's all you need to think of. I'll do the rest.' It was an understatement, but I composed a kind of historical fantasy called *The Elephant* and went to Bristol to take the narrator's part which I have, ever since, where circumstances allowed, grabbed for myself.

Unlike some of the contributors to *Imaginary Conversations*, Watson became a regular radio contributor and he recalls with affection the encouraging atmosphere which prevailed when the features producers foregathered in The Stag, a pub behind Broadcasting House, where 'ideas could be floated of which at least some would reach contract status with the minimum of fuss, under a regime of genial paternalism which to a large extent compensated for unspectacular fees'. It was at this time and within this milieu that Rodgers stumbled upon a new radio form in which radio portraits of contemporary and recently dead writers, like Yeats, were built up from recorded recollections of their friends and contemporaries. This form was to lead Watson to create a mammoth portrait of Gandhi, employing tape-recorded reminiscence. These oral biographies pioneered by Rodgers and the *Imaginary Conversations* series extended the range and use of radio and brought in contributions from people who had previously not attempted to work in this field. Though many of them were not dramatists, the experience of writing such work obviously informed their later approach to work in their preferred fields. Their prose tended afterwards to relate more closely to spoken language but the series in which they participated also had its influence upon later dramatists, who realised, having listened to these conversations, that plays could also be written about such historical figures.

Any account of this period of experiment with new radio forms and of the mastery of the dramatic capacity of the medium by those who wrote and produced feature programmes ought properly to be accompanied by music. At this time, the BBC had something like forty composers on contract, who might be asked on one occasion to write the score for a full-length feature and on another to write some ditty or signature tune for a new chat show. Sometimes the diversity expected was too much for the composer. Anthony Hopkins felt that the experience did not help him develop a style of his own and that the demands were so varied that he became a sort of musical chameleon. But the really great advantage to him was the practical experience of hearing a work very soon after it had been composed. Writing music for concert performance often involves a considerable lapse of time between composition and performance, whereas in the radio studios the lapse of time was only a few days or weeks. William Alwyn also valued this opportunity of working in radio and he is certain that many other composers, such as Britten and Walton and Elizabeth Lutyens, derived enormous benefit from it. He wrote [to author]:

> When working on a feature the collaboration between writer
> and composer was close and intimate – both script and music
> were carefully worked out from the inception of the subject –
> unlike in films where the composer was usually shewn the
> finished film and then asked to write the music. Also the
> composer was encouraged to experiment and to use instru-
> mental or vocal combinations which gave one a further zest for
> work. For example, for one of Louis MacNeice's scripts I used
> two horns only and, for another, a male voice chorus. For
> Bertie Rodgers's *City That Stands On A Hill,* the score was
> composed for solo flute (which I played myself) and a pre-
> recorded choir.

Alwyn also feels that those who commissioned music for films
were often far less imaginative. They expected and insisted upon
music written for a full orchestra when a smaller body of players
would often have been more suitable.

Film music could not afford the delicate variety which radio
invited. It was soon clear to most radio producers that a full
orchestra could very often create the wrong effect. McWhinnie
defines this need to avoid the heavy kind of hand which film
companies expect of their composers.

> The radio composer's main concern is to avoid at all costs any
> feeling of the concert platform; once we associate sound
> patterns with rows of dinner-jacketed instrumentalists we are
> faced with the same clash of conventions which often faces us
> in the theatre.[7]

But there can also be occasions when a full orchestra is needed.
McWhinnie goes on to quote Edward Sackville-West's comments
on the music which Britten wrote for his play *The Rescue.*

> A large ensemble seemed necessary if only because a small one
> is invariably more obtrusive; it is, paradoxically, impossible to
> produce an overall orchestral pianissimo without using a con-
> siderable body of instruments, whereas a double forte requires
> only the minimum.

A full orchestra was certainly suited to the dimensions of *The Rescue*, which was a kind of spoken opera. But on most occasions, for the reasons which McWhinnie gives, it was not suitable and the writers and composers, working hand in glove, had constantly to seek different and varied musical responses. Humphrey Searle, for example, chose music for Gogol's *Diary Of A Madman*, which was scored for violin, cello, clarinet, tenor trombone, Spanish guitar and percussion. The pleasure for the composer in working for radio features was that, as Alwyn assures me, he could experiment continually with different instrumental combinations. This meant that in the fifties in Britain the radio studio became the principal conservatoire. The patronage of the BBC in supporting so many orchestras and musicians meant that there were always people ready to play and work out new ideas. The fact that composers and writers and producers worked in full accord during the making of these radio works also stimulated the creation of new approaches.

Sometimes the composers felt that they were working rather too much as craftsmen performing journeyman's work which prevented them exploiting their personal style. But this journeyman's work was not without its benefits. The composers worked alongside writers and producers like MacNeice and Cleverdon. They found themselves sharing a practical approach which was always guided by technical considerations. It may be supposed by some that this grubbing about in the radio studios served no pure aesthetic purpose and that, for example, MacNeice's art as a poet or Alwyn's as a composer was sullied by this work. Those who presume that the artist must belong to some kind of exalted priesthood naturally believed that this dabbling in the tool-box of radio was aesthetically destructive. But the people involved in radio in Britain at this time would have held to the alternative view of the role and nature of the artist which David Jones expressed so well in his poem *Anathemata*. Commenting upon this poem, Harman Grisewood in his radio talk in 1966 said:

> The purpose of art is not a state of mind but a thing, as tangible and visible as a piece of cake or a pair of stockings. Indeed, Mr Jones insists that the lady in the kitchen or with her needle and thread uses the faculties of the artist, and that in what she is doing she has more in common with Michelangelo or Virgil

than with the patient beaver constructing his dam of twigs across the stream.

Although Jones may have wished that his work had never been dramatised and that he should have had the chance to read the whole of it himself, his view of the artist and of art would have been accepted by most of those who worked in radio. Edward Sackville-West expressed the same view in the prologue to his play *The Rescue:* 'The word *artist* means *joiner* and the artist in radio composition is one who joins things together – words, music, all manner of sounds.'

It was very lucky that so many carpenters, with their diverse interests and extravagant talents, were drawn into the business of composing radio programmes in Britain in the immediate post-war period. Their obsession with the technique of production, with the exact balance of music against words, with the devices of intercutting scenes and of fading voices and effects, was a vital preliminary to the later explosion of dramatic talent which utilised radio and created the second Elizabethan age in the history of British drama.

7.
The Influence of Features

Radio's influence upon dramatic writing in Britain since 1945 has been considerable but it should not be thought that this was always the consequence of conscious intention on the part of the writers or of deliberate policy on the part of the BBC. During the period from 1945 until 1953, when television at last superseded radio as the mass entertainer, most of the important inventive work was written for features rather than drama. Peter Black remarks that in 1946 only three plays were written for radio and that there was only one play in 1947 and two in 1948.[1] Radio drama thrived at this time as a national repertory theatre supplying its audiences with a repertory of stage plays for which there was tremendous public demand. The only dramatic innovations at this time were contributed by writers of serials like *The Robinson Family*, *Mrs Dale's Diary*, *The Archers* and *Dick Barton*. The serial had been an American and Australian innovation and *The Robinson Family* had been introduced during the war by Alan Melville as a propaganda vehicle on the BBC's Overseas Service. *Mrs Dale's Diary*, which was the inspiration of Jonquil Anthony and Ted Willis, had the objective of mirroring the provincial life of the middle class while Godfrey Baseley's *The Archers* was to give townsmen a whiff of life on the farm. None of these serials had any intellectual pretensions but their daily broadcasting was to create some interesting effects. The Archer family and the world of Mrs Dale, the doctor's wife, were to become as real to many listeners as the life that went on around them. The listeners here contributed with their imagination to the point at which they actually believed in the existence of these serial characters. They also caused some changes in the original format of the serials. When Mrs Dale first opened her diary, she was surrounded by servants and minions who were portrayed only as comic figures, but in 1962 she was suddenly uprooted from her smart suburb and dumped in a new town where her husband became a member of a group practice in the National Health Service. The Archers, who began as Mummerset figures, also moved closer to reality as the serial continued.

But the serial did not permit very much innovation or stretch of the imagination and it could not be said that it inspired any budding dramatists. Nor, at this time, did the Drama department do very much for young playwrights. Black observes that the difficulty which faced Gielgud at this time was rather similar to the one which had faced him in 1930.

> Plays were hugely popular but the audience wanted what they knew and liked. Within this convention drama flourished – the audience for Saturday Night Theatre a steady round ten million – and created its own company of masters of aural acting, bearing names as distinguished as any in the theatre.

To satisfy such a popular demand, it was still necessary to serve up the accepted diet of plays and it is ironic that a greater contribution was made to the evolution of new dramatic forms by the Features department under Gilliam, who once observed that no radio service can survive on a diet of classics and that it must initiate or die. Gilliam's brief was to continue the provision of the wide range of documentary and current affairs programmes which had served his audience during the war. But in the course of providing this wartime fare, producers like Dillon, MacNeice and Sieveking had already worked out new ways of dramatising such documentary material. As has already been described, they had begun by using music merely as an embellishment and had then learned, in collaboration with composers, how to create a dramatic form which was particular to radio. A good example of this particular form from this period is Dillon's *Rumpelstiltskin*, for which Collinson wrote the music and which was to win the first Radio Italia Prize in 1949. Dillon would still persist in calling it a feature but it is, in effect, a kind of spoken opera, in which the speech is counterpointed by the music. It owes its structure to the narrative style of the documentary and does not contain a tightly worked out dramatic plot but is, for all that, a dramatisation of the story of Rumpelstiltskin. The kind of picture-making which this kind of radio work involved naturally attracted many writers of note who did not regard themselves as dramatists.

Occasionally such writers felt the need, like Dylan Thomas, to create a dramatic plot but there were producers like Cleverdon who would then reassure them that they need not employ the Aristotelian form. The pattern of the feature encouraged the telling of a story in sequence with dramatic inserts as illustrations of the theme in a manner which resembled to some extent the form of the novel. But while it could therefore appeal to the novelist it naturally invited the contributions of journalists attempting summaries of recent history. But the treatment of such recent events in programmes like Hugh Trevor-Roper's *The Last Days of Hitler*, Chester Wilmot's *The Battle Of Britain* and John Hersey's adaptation of his book *Hiroshima* also suggested similar treatment of more remote history. A series called *News From Yesterday* permitted the journalistic on-the-spot method of reportage to describe events like the Battle of Waterloo and the Great Fire of London. A form of autobiography was also developed in a series called *A Year To Remember*, in which, for example, Compton Mackenzie recalled 1901, Rose Macaulay described 1913 and Olivia Manning recaptured life in Greece in 1940–1. In the meantime, MacNeice's experience had also taught him that poets could make good use of this radio form and in the BBC Year Book for 1947 he invited his fellow poets to join him, assuring them that they could achieve things through the medium which were worth while and unique. His own work proves that he here had in mind the use which the poet could make of a medium which did not invite self-indulgent word play but an extreme verbal economy enlightened by telling imagery. The creation of the Third Programme had enlarged the opportunity for poetry readings but MacNeice had less interest in this kind of literary contribution than in the exercising of the poetic mind in features. Under the direction of Gilliam, writers of all kinds were encouraged to contribute and the range of subjects thought suitable was now enormously enlarged.

Another series, *Return Journey*, which also made use of writers who were not dramatists by trade, involved Sean O'Faolain in a return to Cork and Henry Reed on a similar journey to Naples. Reed, who had been drawn to radio by the example of

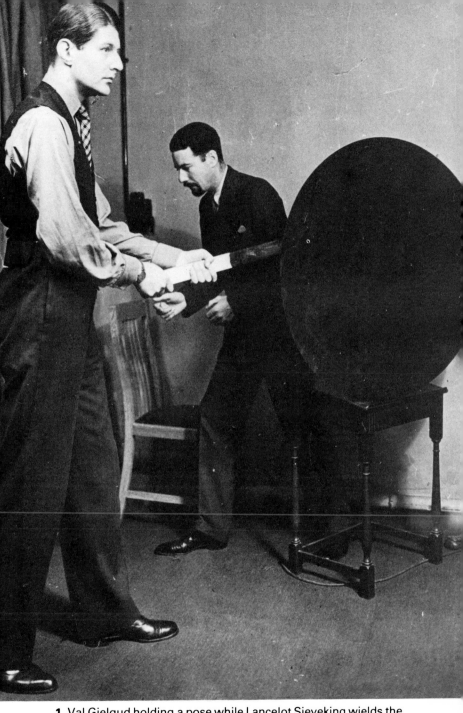

1. Val Gielgud holding a pose while Lancelot Sieveking wields the fading board in the first rehearsal of a television play in June, 1930. *(BBC Copyright)*

2(a) Louis MacNeice, directing a play in 1946. *(BBC Hulton Picture Library)*

2(b) D.G. Bridson in 1949. *(BBC Copyright)*

3. Francis Dillon in action, 1947. *(BBC Copyright)*

4. Tyrone Guthrie directing rehearsals of his play *Top of the Ladder* at the St James's Theatre, London, in 1950. *(BBC Hulton Picture Library)*

5. Laurence Gilliam at his desk in 1953 with Features producer, Alan Burgess. *(BBC Copyright)*

6(a) The BBC Radiophonic Workshop in 1958, which specialised in the construction of new sounds derived from natural sounds or everyday noises. *(BBC Copyright)*

6(b) The studio control room in 1979 during the recording of a play. *(BBC Copyright)*

7(a) Giles Cooper listening to Gladys Young (Mrs Corney) and Wilfred Downing (Oliver Twist) performing his serial adaptation *Oliver Twist,* by Charles Dickens, in 1952. *(BBC Copyright)*

7(b) Frederick Raphael playing a part in his dramatised feature *The Daedalus Dimension* for Radio 3 in 1978. On his right are Nigel Stock and Joseph O'Conor. *(BBC Copyright)*

8. Donald McWhinnie and Samuel Beckett in one of their necessary huddles. The occasion was the television production of *Ghost Trio*. *(Christina Burton)*

MacNeice's *The Dark Tower*, quickly became a radio addict. This addiction was to lead him to exploit a variety of forms and there is no doubt that his work served as an inspiration to many younger writers. Reed is probably best known for his very amusing satires devoted to the life and times of his twelve-tone composer, Hilda Tablet, but some of his other work also deserves attention and assessment. Cleverdon, for example, considers that these witty satires are not the equal of *The Unblest* and *The Monument*, two verse plays devoted to the Italian poet, Giacomo Leopardi, or of his *Streets Of Pompeii* and his *Vincenzo*, which portrayed Vincenzo Gonzaga, Duke of Mantua. Other important contributions made by Reed were his radio adaptations of Melville's *Moby Dick* and Hardy's *The Dynasts*, which he presented in a six-part serial. He was later to put his knowledge of Italian to good use by translating the plays of Pirandello and Ugo Betti, some of which thus had their British *premières* on radio and not on the stage. Reed's eventual contribution was that of a playwright and translator of plays but it was in radio and in features that he first found an outlet for his imagination. It was in the same congenial milieu that Pamela Hansford-Johnson was encouraged to develop the original formula of Heppenstall's *Imaginary Conversations*. Under Gilliam's slogan that radio must initiate or die, she was encouraged to create a dialogue not between historical characters but between the characters in Proust's *A La Recherche Du Temps Perdu* with the object of throwing further light on them. It might be thought that such a work ought more properly to have been stimulated by the Drama department but the fact that it was a Features production merely underlines the spirit of experiment and ingenuity which then informed work in features.

It should be no surprise that for something like five years following the institution of the Radio Italia prizes the BBC nominated features rather than plays and that many of them won prizes.

It has sometimes been supposed that this monopoly of creative effort in radio was entirely due to the inspiration of Gilliam and his producers but other factors contributed. While television had supplanted radio as the mass medium in the USA, relegating radio to the task of supplying disc-jockey programmes interspersed with news bulletins, British radio still had to provide the range of programmes it had broadcast during the war. The failure to develop portable tape-recording equipment made feature production dependent upon written scripts which could be enlivened by specially written music performed by the very large number of musicians in regular employment at the BBC. It is true that wire-recording had existed for some time but this system did not lend itself to editing and proved too clumsy for the purposes of copying excerpts from existing disc-recordings. The construction of feature programmes therefore remained the task of writers and of producers with some literary talent. Their task was not to make a play of the events and social debates which were the subject of their features but to present material in a dramatic fashion which might otherwise not be thought attractive. This dramatisation to serve what was often a journalistic purpose was naturally free of some of the constraints which the dramatist would have had to observe. Just as writers like MacNeice practised considerable ingenuity in containing directions as to movement and change of scene within the dialogue, the feature writer could also desert dramatic conventions and rely when needed upon the simple narration and linking voice. But in the course of serving the need to communicate via radio, the dramatic devices employed pointed towards ways in which the radio play and eventually the theatre play could be effectively altered.

It was the writers who were listening and learning at this time from the examples of the radio feature but few of them found it easy to persuade Gielgud's Drama department to accept their proposals. It had not in any case yet become the custom for any aspiring dramatist to submit his or her work to the radio before trying a theatre, and Peter Shaffer, who in 1944 at the age of eighteen submitted his first play, *The Murder of Pamphilius Prawn*, only to have it rejected, was quite a rarity.

Shaffer had to wait until 1957 for his radio debut with *The Prodigal Father* at a time when the Drama department had become more receptive to new ideas. But in the immediate post-war period, when there was a bias in favour of the immediately acceptable and the BBC did not wish to cause too much offence, it was not always easy for even established playwrights to get their plays broadcast. Some theatre plays were rejected for the good reason that they could not be easily adapted to the medium or because they had been specifically written for the West End theatre and its rather special audience. Though Emlyn Williams, for example, succeeded in gaining a radio performance of *Pepper and Sand* in 1947, his pre-war plays *A Murder Has Been Arranged* and *The Morning Star* were both turned down. In 1946 John Whiting submitted *Paul Southman* which was rejected on the grounds that it was thought to have an unpleasant flavour. In 1949 he had better luck with *Eye Witness* and was so delighted with Martin C. Webster's production of it that he immediately offered *Love's Old Sweet Song*, only to have it rejected. In 1951 he offered *Saint's Day*, which owes something to the earlier *Paul Southman*, and it was rejected on the grounds that it was thought to be too theatrical. It was not until 1961 that the BBC made amends for the rejection of Whiting's masterpiece when the play was included in a series entitled *From The Fifties*.

American playwrights also had their difficulties. In 1951 Arthur Miller's *Death Of A Salesman* was turned down for the extraordinary reason that it was thought to be of limited appeal. The play had to wait until 1959 before it was broadcast. When the BBC sought to repeat the production in the following year and also to undertake a production of *The Crucible*, Miller refused. His trials with the BBC cannot be compared to those which Eugene O'Neill suffered, although it has to be said in fairness that O'Neill brought most of the trouble on himself. In 1928 the BBC had wanted to do a radio production of *The Emperor Jones* when Paul Robeson happened to be available in London to play the lead. O'Neill, like many theatre playwrights at that time, feared that exposure on radio would damage the play's chances in the theatre.He therefore demanded a fee of £1000, which he must have known the BBC could not afford. Gielgud went on trying to persuade O'Neill to change his mind and in 1937 the playwright relented only to change his mind at the last moment. It was not until 1959, more than thirty years after the BBC's original proposal, that the play was eventually broadcast in a brilliant production by John Gibson. Compared with O'Neill, Clifford Odets only suffered a relatively short period of delay when his *Golden Boy* was submitted in March 1938 but was not performed until 1950. Another mystifying delay afflicted Robert Bolt's *A Man For All Seasons*, which he originally submitted in 1951. He was advised that he ought to extend the trial scene and that he ought to tidy up the opening scene which was thought to contain too much historical scene-setting. The play languished in the in-tray for four years and then Bolt wrote asking to have his copy back as a theatre was then interested in staging it. Donald McWhinnie was to make amends for this rather off-hand treatment of the play with his brilliant production of Bolt's *The Drunken Sailor*.

Cleverdon's comment on this treatment of young playwrights and foreign playwrights of distinction is that Gielgud's attitude towards avant-garde dramatists had always been cautious, if not hostile. His earlier disagreement with Guthrie gives some support for this view but Michael Bakewell, who was to join the Script department when McWhinnie had become deputy head of Drama and who was one of those who assisted McWhinnie in the dramatic revolution which began in 1953, makes a more balanced judgement. Gielgud was committed to a theatre which was noble and grandiose and he simply could not understand the style of play which the writers, responding to radio, were beginning to construct. It has been the custom to denigrate Gielgud's regime and to deplore the eventual destruction of Gilliam's Features department but it has also to be said that Gilliam resisted change too. The obvious technical advantages of the portable tape-recorder were at first deliberately ignored. This machine argued for a complete change in the manner of composing features. It at last allowed the voices of the people, whose shouts and murmurs Harding had championed in Manchester in the thirties, to be heard perfectly and exactly. It could be used to copy musical excerpts, dispensing with the need for the presence of orchestras in the studios. It argued the greater use of ingenious cutting and editing and gave the producer, rather than the writer, much more editorial control. It ought to have been welcomed but for some time it was carefully ignored. Michael Barsley recalls using such a machine to make a programme in 1950 but the programme he made was never broadcast. Rene Cutforth, who had been covering the Korean War for the BBC, had used a Japanese portable tape-recorder when he was a war correspondent. It was very cumbersome and weighed twenty-four pounds. He imagined when he returned to London in 1952 that his colleagues would be eager to use it and was somewhat surprised when this alarming gadget was locked away in a cupboard. Despite all the imaginative work which had been instigated by Gilliam and his colleagues, the portable tape-recorder was regarded with suspicion and hostility. Its arrival, which argued a totally new approach to the making of features, happened to coincide with the realisation that the growing popularity of television argued the virtual disbandment of the Features department. It seems to have been thought that it was bad enough to surrender the field of documentary and current affairs programmes to television but worse to have to contemplate the use of a machine which implied another kind of internal revolution.

This distaste for the new gadget is perhaps understandable. Writers, composers, producers, actors and musicians had evolved a complex and very fruitful creative relationship. Composers had derived considerable stimulus from working with spoken words as well as music and when the tape-recorder came in they were no longer needed in the same way. The style of working which involved writers as editors of their material during the course of production had been enormously valuable. The tape-recorder meant that this collaborating community of different talents would no longer be needed. The exchanges between producers, writers and composers had not only produced masterpieces like Sackville-West's *The Rescue* for which Britten wrote the music, but also the collections of folk songs, which were first treated by Dillon in his wartime series *Country Magazine* and which then became the subject of specially constructed features by people like David Thomson, W. R. Rodgers and Alan Lomax.

Rodgers introduced a new radio form in *The Bare Stones of Aran* which made use of folk stories enlivened by music, and David Thomson followed this with Scottish studies like *Black House Into White* and *Sons Of The Sea*. This method of interrelating stories and music was to lead Rodgers to develop a new form of radio biography, the radio portrait in which people who had, for example, known Joyce or Yeats contributed their reminiscences. It was also to lead to programmes devoted entirely to folk music, like Maurice Brown's *East Anglia Sings* and his *Saintes Maries Gypsy Festival* and to the engagement again of Alan Lomax, who contributed, among other programmes, a series of eight one-hour pieces on the folk music of Italy.

The great virtue of this era in British radio was its readiness to consider almost any subject worthy of study; the role of its pro-

ducers, who were both poets and scholars, was also extremely
important in coping with both the popular and the esoteric. There
is no doubt that on occasion the British radio feature employed a
rather false rhetoric and trumpets were sometimes sounded too
frequently. It has been thought by Black and others that the
decline of this department was wholly due to the BBC's need to
economise and to direct its documentary effort into television.
But this is to neglect the technical effects of the introduction of
the tape-recorder which rendered the previous method of composition unnecessary and disposed of the need for the poetic and
allusive narrative. The portable tape-recorder invited a much
tighter selection of material and reduced the narrator to the role of
a journalist linking the quotations. It also encouraged the use
of the wholly impromptu statement and at last relegated the
specially written script performed by the contributor or by an
actor. It was this development which paradoxically was to lead to
the renaissance of British drama in the late fifties, when all of the
energy which had once characterised Gilliam's department was
to be found at last in Gielgud's drama studios.

But before this occurred there were one or two dramatists
picking their way towards this eventual development. It is
perhaps no accident that one of them was Giles Cooper, whose
Irish origins played some part in determining a method of
composition which was attuned to the manners of speech in a
way was not then customary on the British stage. Cooper was
never to write dramatic parts to be performed in the accepted
theatrical sense.

His experience as an actor also encouraged him to employ a
style of dialogue which was extremely economic and which
depended for interpretation upon the performance of the actors.
In this particular reliance upon the capacity of the actors to
interpret the parts, Cooper was in advance of his time and many
directors found his spare dialogue perplexing. Like many other
playwrights who were to emerge in the next ten years, Cooper
also provided some unintentional mystification because it was
not immediately clear to some readers and producers what his
message was. It was at this time the custom for a play to have
some message concealed beneath the surface of the dialogue and
the apparent action. But Cooper's plays, as Michael Bakewell
once put it, were only about what they appeared to be about.

They were about the things which you could hear the characters discussing. In some of his later plays, Cooper betrays a gentle satirical view of the plight of middle-class man surrounded by the apparatus and trappings of an industrial consumer society. But several of his critics have not been satisfied with this surface message and have tended to look deeper. When he submitted his first play which was called *The Trinbino Craze*, the BBC's readers were understandably mystified. The play involved a Mr Baloobin who buys up a lot of left-hand gloves and then invents a game in order to sell them to a gullible public. The play was not about anything else but the readers were worried because they feared that it might contain some dark hidden message.

If Cooper had been merely a writer and not an actor in close contact with the radio community and the theatre, he might well have postponed writing further plays for some time. But he was lucky in that while he continued writing his own plays he was able to get commissions to adapt works like Dickens's *Oliver Twist* and David Haworth's *One Night In Styria* for radio. This journeyman work was undoubtedly helpful. It persuaded the drama readers and producers that he was possessed of some competence but it also assisted him in the practice of converting the narrative of the novel to the dramatic form. Dramatists like Cooper had to make a somewhat furtive approach to radio at this time because their work did not fit the fashion.

Another Irish writer who was to contribute some important work to radio drama was H. A. L. Craig, who actually began his radio apprenticeship as a cricket commentator assisting John Arlott. Like Cooper, who continued working occasionally as an actor, Craig also worked as a journalist and literary reviewer while occasionally managing to write radio features on people like Raleigh, Chatterton and Raymond Chandler. It was really much easier for writers like Craig to find employment of this kind at this time than it was for dramatists like Cooper, who was offering a style of play which was not yet appreciated. But the contribution which writers made to the creation of feature programmes was to have its influence upon the later development of the radio play and, in time, upon the theatre play. The discipline of the radio feature, which enjoyed in Britain a survival into an age which in the USA had become already dominated by television, encouraged an approach to dramatic structure which had no place in the theatre at that time. Its speech, like the dialogue of Cooper's plays, depended to some extent upon the subtle interpretations brought to it by the actors.

But the portable tape-recorder was to change this approach and it was to become one of the tools of the radio trade at the very moment when British radio lost its mass audience. The necessary curtailment of the Features department and the departure of many of its producers, like Michael Barsley, into television, brought this particular artistic venture to an end. The portable tape-recorder was not favoured by some of the old hands in radio features but it was to have an effect upon the dramatists which has not been sufficiently appreciated.

8.
The Discovery of Silence

In the nineteenth century the camera suddenly revealed the nature of light. This revelation immediately had an effect upon the work of the Impressionist painters. A somewhat similar effect was created by the evidence presented by the portable tape-recorder, which suddenly made writers aware of the realities of ordinary speech and of the nature of silence. Recordings of ordinary people speaking had been available since the mid-thirties but on most occasions such recordings were confined to presenting rather formal statements of opinion and they tended not to include the hesitations and murmurs which are to be found in ordinary conversation. The people who made such contributions tended to speak in a rather stilted and well-behaved manner so that the listener could only get a very vague impression of how they might speak in ordinary conversation. But when the portable tape-recorder made it possible to take the equivalent of the camera shot of ordinary conversation, conducted by people who were no longer being made self-conscious by the presence of the machine, the nature of speech and of its silences was at last revealed.

In Britain this revelation began to have its impact upon the writers in the mid-fifties. It would be wrong to give the impression that these writers all bought portable tape-recorders or that they listened continually to documentary programmes which included recorded inserts of ordinary speech. Many writers at the time were probably not consciously aware of the model of speech which the tape-recorder presented but it was often enough for a writer to hear only a snatch of such a recording for him or her to alter the manner of dialogue. The evidence presented by the tape-recorder made the writers listen with fresh ears to ordinary speech. Some of them immediately realised that it was not enough to write dramatic parts accompanied by sparse directions as to the manner of delivery. The emulation of natural speech in dramatic dialogue required much careful notation. It was not merely necessary to indicate where characters should pause before speaking. It was essential to determine the exact pace of speech exchanges.

This response to the revelation of real speech and the silences within it was not consciously realised by the writers at the time. It was a response which was guided less by any philosophical consideration than by a sense of craftsmanship. Their ears had been focused to attend the phenomena of ordinary speech and conversation. They became sharply aware that the previous manner of presenting dialogue was very inaccurate and that the way of presenting spoken language on the stage was totally artificial. It was no longer merely a matter of objecting to the stage dialects which presumed to approximate to Cockney or Mummerset or Northern. It was realised that the written dialogue was itself at fault. Dramatic dialogue did not pay attention to the *longueurs* and hesitations. It took little account, for example, of the way in which a person after a long pause may say 'No', when the meaning of this utterance may in fact be 'Maybe' or even on some occasions 'Yes'.

There was suddenly this need to present an image of actual conversation rather than the portrayal of accepted stage dialogue. It followed that plays which had been written in this manner and which then appeared in the theatre had also to be accompanied by meticulous directions not only as to speech but as to the movements of the actors. Playwrights like Pinter and Beckett were no longer satisfied with the accepted forms of stage direction which presumed that interpretation of the script should be only the concern of the producer or director. They began to look upon the business of constructing a play more in the manner of a composer of music. They were not merely concerned with accurate representation of dialect but with the question of pace. It was suddenly appreciated by the writers that they had to exercise more control over their works in production. David Rudkin typifies this approach in preferring the word 'legislation' to 'stage direction' to describe his instructions as to the manner of performance.

This new approach to the structure and timing of dialogue and to the very precise control of sound effects and movement was initiated entirely by the writers. Theatre directors and managements in Britain were generally rather mystified by this new style and it is no accident that many of the new playwrights in the mid-fifties found more immediate understanding in the radio studios, where people like McWhinnie and Bakewell were already acquainted with the evidence offered by the tape-recorder. But when these plays were first rehearsed and broadcast, it has to be said that even some of the very experienced radio actors were slightly bemused by them. Scripts which dictated every grunt and murmur and stipulated precisely the length of every pause and hesitation evoked a crop of Green Room jokes. One favourite actors' sally at this time was: 'Is this a long pause, old boy, or is it a short pause? Or is it paws?' As this question indicates, the use of the word 'pause' was soon found by the writers to be too vague and Beckett was one of the first to start using dots instead of pauses to indicate the length of such hesitations. There was as a result an apocryphal story about Beckett once rebuking an actor for pausing for only three dots instead of four. Though these actors' jokes may seem trivial they serve to record the impact of this new form of script notation which sought to make dramatic dialogue simulate the newly perceived nature of ordinary speech and the silences it often contained.

Writers became obsessed by the need to present their intentions clearly and precisely. Alun Owen recalls meeting Pinter during this period in a great state of excitement because he had just decided to go over from pauses to dots. Owen was someone who could well appreciate Pinter's excitement. His first play, *Two Sons*, was not in fact composed by being written down. The play involved a man from Liverpool and one from Wales, and Owen, an actor by upbringing, actually performed the dialogue and recorded it. He then played the recordings back and wrote the lines down. He did not merely dictate the lines; he acted them out, giving them the manners of speech which he envisaged the actors employing.

As a one-time actor, Owen, like Cooper, naturally had an ear which was attuned to the likely performance of his lines. But he was at last inhabiting again a milieu in which the ancient manners of oral composition had been revived. To such writers the

rhetoric of the set speech was anathema and the primary objective was the meticulous presentation of the speech of ordinary
people involved in everyday matters. It has sometimes been
supposed that this redirection of interest towards the trivia and
commonplace of ordinary speech was a response generated by
political and philosophical considerations on the part of the
writers. This assumption on the part of critics and interpreters of
these new plays derives from the accepted belief that a writer is
always seeking to say something more than may appear to be
present on the surface and that he is concealing other meanings
and intentions. As the plays often displayed social derelicts and
lost souls it became easy to conclude that such work had some
socio-political aim. But it has to be said that the writers in the
fifties and sixties who wrote these very socially observant plays
had widely differing political and philosophical views and that
the only common factor was their response to the evidence of the
portable tape-recorder. The revelation of the nuances of ordinary
speech brought about a rejection of what Wordsworth in the
Preface to *The Lyrical Ballads* had pilloried as poetic diction. The
objective of the dramatists was to reject all verbal banquets and to
concentrate entirely upon the economies observed in ordinary
speech. Two off-the-cuff remarks by Hemingway, that good
writers write it how it is and that the art of writing lies in knowing
what to leave out, were much quoted by British dramatists at this
time. For whereas it had been previously presumed by artists and
intellectuals that people not given to the use of many words did
not communicate anything of significance, it was now appreciated that they did in fact communicate. In order to emulate this
economic communication in few words, the dramatists rejected
the rich hyperbole and the grand manner. Though they were not
consciously seeking to equal Wordsworth's ambition to represent
that 'plainer and more emphatic language' in order to approach
and describe feelings which Wordsworth described as being 'less
under the action of social vanity', the effects of their approach
to the problems of diction were to be somewhat similar. In his
Preface, Wordsworth wrote:

Low and rustic life was generally chosen because in that situation the essential passions of the heart find a better soil in
which they can attain their maturity, are less under restraint,

and speak a plainer, more emphatic, language; because in that situation our elementary feelings exist in a state of greater simplicity and consequently may be more accurately contemplated and more forcibly communicated; because the manners of rural life germinate from those elementary feelings and from the necessary character of rural occupations are more easily comprehended; and are more durable; and, lastly, because in that situation the passions of men are incorporated with the beautiful and permanent forms of nature.

It is not, of course, the case that dramatists in Britain in the fifties and sixties were inspired by Wordsworth's romantic notion that truth may only lie at the bottom of a rustic well. It is, further, arguable that Wordsworth did not quite achieve what he set out to do when he applied his philosophical notions to the matter of writing poetry. What happened to British dramatists is a practice to match his theory, these dramatists stumbled upon their contemporary equivalents of 'low and rustic life' and then sought to imitate the 'plainer, more emphatic, language' without being possessed in advance of any particular theory about the 'passions of the heart' finding a purer form of expression.

This pursuit of a dramatic diction which closely resembled the realities of ordinary speech led naturally to a choice of characters who were liable to use unadorned speech. The linguistic interest was paramount and the characters were not chosen in advance or to accord with any socio-political or philosophical considerations. There were certainly some dramatists like David Mercer, who began as a writer of television plays and whose Marxist convictions determined the shape and direction of the debate contained within his plays, but, like all his contemporaries, he adhered to the same meticulous observation of speech manners and movement accompanying silences. The dramatists, whose ears had been alerted to the nature of the silences in ordinary conversation and the way in which they could contain the unspoken thought and be the void where the emotional tension rested, naturally wrote in a style which was unlike the accepted theatrical fashion. They no longer wrote recognisable 'parts' with set speeches, which could then be handed over for interpretation by the actors and directors. They were no longer presenting a theatrical formula containing a debate on social or political issues.

They were writing as close as possible to the kind of speech their ears had been trained to hear in the streets and the shops and the pubs.

John Osborne's play *Look Back In Anger*, which was socially significant and theatrically successful, is sometimes associated with this revolution in dramatic diction and structure. The play's hero was an Angry Young Man and his presence was socially significant because it was the first appearance of such a figure on the West End stage. It now provides a dramatic footnote to social history in a manner similar to Restoration comedy recording the arrival of the *nouveaux riches* in London's society of fops. It records the arrival of the provincial Angry Young Man but its theatrical style, despite its subject, is one which would have been acceptable to Noel Coward. The hero speaks with a provincial accent which ought to be close to Birmingham, but this accent needs only to be a caricature rather than a closely observed tape copy of Birmingham speech. The style of Osborne's play is not anywhere near the style of the plays of Pinter or Cooper. It exploits the accepted theatrical conventions and makes its social point quite explicitly.

The fact that it deals with the arrival of the Angry Young Man, a term which its West End audiences could well have applied to some of the new provincial playwrights, should not lead to the confusion of associating this play with those which were written in the new form of dramatic diction. Its success did not depend upon exact observation of every grunt and murmur; it was a play which presumed performances on the part of the actors which would project the characters and demonstrate them in the accepted West End manner.

Osborne's play was socially important as well as being theatrically successful but, from an artistic point of view, it properly belongs to the style of drama which was now being questioned by many of his contemporaries. In the context of Wordsworth's argument in favour of the speech of low and rustic life, *Look Back In Anger* is in the same category as Thomas's *Under Milk Wood*, which deliberately exploited a high poetic style. It employs the kind of poetic diction which Wordsworth wished to desert in favour of a more simplified form. Despite the debt which *Under Milk Wood* owes to the structure of the radio feature, its language does not pretend to be an exact copy of ordinary speech. The lines are written to be declaimed and sounded in a manner which is meant to be larger than life. It naturally takes good account of the musical ingenuities of Welsh English but it voices in a rhetorical manner what the people of Llaregyb are thinking and does not pretend to depict what they might actually say in real life. Thomas, as a poet, employs a torrent of words to paint a picture in the mind which is significantly marred when the play is seen on a stage as opposed to being heard on radio. The manner of his play is quite different from the manner of the dramatists, whose ears had been focused afresh by the evidence of the tape-recorder.

To place Thomas's *Under Milk Wood* and Osborne's *Look Back In Anger,* which served different theatrical purposes, on one side of a divide in dramatic diction and in opposition to Beckett's *All That Fall* or Pinter's *The Caretaker* or Cooper's *Mathry Beacon* may seem rather arbitrary. The purpose is not to make a negative judgment of these plays by Osborne and Thomas. Both of them in their respective ways were highly successful and artistically competent. But the linguistic and dramatic style which they employ is consonant with the accepted conventions of their time. This style, which presumes a certain manner of presentation and performance, is in sharp contrast to the style chosen by their immediate contemporaries who effected a revolution in dramatic diction and structure. These two plays are not to be overheard in the manner demanded by Pinter or Cooper. They present an object to be admired and received which is dependent upon its successful reception through traditional theatrical styles of projected performance. It is important to draw a line between these two plays and the plays which followed them in order to display the differences created by this revolution in dramatic diction.

The origin of this revolution may easily be traced to the ideas which became established in British radio studios but there were some other influences at work in the French theatre during the same period. The limited access to French radio which French writers had long endured and accepted had deflected the innovators and pioneers of new forms of expression towards the novel and the film. The French film industry, unlike its British equivalent, had for a long time encouraged talents of artistic and intellectual quality and, while radio remained in Britain the only form in which dramatic experiment was possible, the French film offered French writers an equivalent ground for experiment. An awareness of the evidence presented by the tape-recorder was also present in France and it first made an impact in the dialogue of French films, which necessarily required a colloquial form. The lessons learned here soon found expression in novels written by those who were described as a *nouvelle vague*. These novelists brought into question the traditional formality of French literary and dramatic expression and their influence soon made itself felt in the theatre. It can be said that certain philosophical motivations promoted this development and that Sartre's Existentialism played some part in the formation of their ideas.

The vogue of interest in the ideas of Logical Positivism has also been cited as a stimulus but all such philosophical explanations neglect the compulsion felt on the part of the writers to break away from the accepted styles of literary and dramatic composition in a country where there had been an even stricter insistence upon the merits of formal expression than had been the case in Britain. French writers, who had also been made aware of the true nature of spoken language and of the silences which surrounded the words, no longer wished to be read solely upon the page. The narratives of the novels of the *nouvelle vague*, whose British contemporaries were largely to be found in radio studios, invited the reader to read them aloud and their dialogues closely imitated the patterns of ordinary speech. It had become more important to demonstrate how people said things than to present argued debates.

The French example was eventually to play an important part in easing the way for new dramatists in Britain. Because its aims and interests were similar and because British intellectuals have always held the French model in great esteem, established critics began slowly to concede that these plays which prompted the actors to make jokes about dots and pauses might, after all, have some merit. But understandably they had to find respectable intellectual explanations and confusion was furthered when they resorted to associating this revolution in dramatic diction and structure with a variety of socio-political ideas and philosophies. Luckily, nobody added to the confusion by suggesting that the writers were inspired by reading Wordsworth's Preface to the *Lyrical Ballads*. It would be very misleading to suggest that they were, but in retrospect the conflict between what Wordsworth called poetic diction and the romantic poetry he sought to write provides a parallel which can assist our understanding of what happened during the fifties

Wordsworth approached this problem of changing literary diction from the opposite direction to the one taken by the fifties dramatists. He presumed that a purer truth was to be found in low and rustic life and he then gave it an imagined voice. But the writers in France and Britain in the fifties heard the voices first and then sought means to set them in credible surroundings. The classic stage set of the British theatre in the thirties, the drawing-room with its inevitable French windows back of stage, was totally unsuitable. To the bewilderment of those who had become accustomed to this kind of set, the new plays were sited casually in public parks, in lodging-houses and in pubs. The pursuit of closely observed colloquial speech demanded settings and venues which had none of the formality previously accepted in the theatre. But it also argued an imitation of the economies of ordinary speech, which, it was now appreciated, contained more subtleties and depths than had previously been thought. The grand phrases and set speeches which Wordsworth would have described as poetic diction were now suspect. The emphasis was on economy of words and on the bare statement.

In Britain, the beginnings of this revolution are to be found in the early fifties, when, for example, Cooper was already writing in this style. His early plays were understandably difficult to accept and when he submitted *The Man Who Went Nowhere* in 1951 the BBC drama readers were slightly mystified. They thought it a strange play. It had the merit of being specially and competently written for radio. It was thought to be about something, but what that something was, was difficult to determine. Cooper, like many other writers who followed in his wake, frequently suffered this kind of reaction. Because his plays did not present a recognisable debate, a theatrical argument set either in tragic or comic terms, those who were trained in the traditional style could not satisfactorily explain them. But they were largely looking in the wrong direction. They were, as it were, looking at the plays instead of listening to them. Their ears were not yet as trained as those of the writers. And the writers, consciously and un-consciously, had been exposed to a diet of actuality recordings which began even before the tape-recorder made such material so explicit. As early as 1947, for example, the specialist in the collection of bird-song, Ludwig Koch, had offered feature programmes like *Sounds Of A Summer Evening* and *Sunday Morning in Petticoat Lane*, which presented a medley of camera snapshots of ordinary life.

The fact that the speech in such features was often in dialect was no longer the only significant revelation. Many of the new writers were themselves of provincial origin and did not speak or wish to acquire Oxford English accents. It was not therefore the demonstration of dialect speech which appealed; it was the presentation of the fact that matters of importance could be communicated in this speech which had been presumed simple and uncouth. When the tape-recorder dispensed with the need for scripted and performed speech and provided the living reality at any time of day, in news reports as well as in documentaries, the writers began to respond to this compelling need to represent the speech they heard in their dramatic dialogue. Some of these writers who had previously worked on features were brought much more directly to face the evidence provided by the tape-recorder. They now took part in the process of cutting and editing real speech and became actively aware of its inconsistencies and ambiguities and of the meanings which are sometimes contained within its hesitations and its silences. This awareness was to lead to the creation of works like *June Evening* by Bill Naughton, which was produced by Cleverdon and recalled a day in the life of a Lancashire street in 1921 during the miners' Lock-Out. The microphone hung above the street, popping in and out of the small houses, heard old women dream and complain and the miners cursing their hard times, and witnessed the birth of a baby in a house with a leaking roof. This play employed a device similar to that which Cleverdon had advised Thomas to use in his *Under Milk Wood*, whereby the listener is persuaded that the microphone is eavesdropping on a community. But Naughton came much closer to the actual speech of his Lancashire miners, giving the dramatic impression that they had actually been recorded. This kind of very close representation of ordinary speech was one of the consequences of being able at last to hear the reality of ordinary speech recorded on tape. Writers and producers working with this recorded material to create features naturally came closest of all to an awareness of the realities of spoken language.

It was a lucky coincidence that in 1953, at the very moment when the writers were becoming aware of this need for a different emphasis involving a change in dramatic diction and structure, Donald McWhinnie was made deputy to Val Gielgud in the Radio Drama department at the BBC. At the same time there were some significant changes in the Script department which receives and filters unsolicited plays. It was placed in the hands of Barbara Bray with Eric Ewens as her assistant, and Michael Bakewell also joined the team. Like McWhinnie, Bray and Ewens had considerable radio experience and they were sympathetic to the new writing which began to come in. McWhinnie and his colleagues were more than qualified as radio drama producers. In 1950 McWhinnie had translated Carl Zuckmayer's *The Captain of Kopenick* for a radio production and in 1952 he had collaborated with Frank Hauser, the Oxford Playhouse producer, in an adaptation for radio of Henry James's *Portrait Of A Lady*. He was later (1957) to translate Gerhart Hauptmann's *Elga* and to adapt a number of other works, including Joyce Cary's *The Horse's Mouth*, Kafka's *The Castle*, William Golding's *Free Fall* and James Hanley's *Levine*. At a time when television had at last replaced radio as the mass medium in Britain, radio drama was freed from some of the constraints which had made people like Gielgud rather cautious in commissioning unusual or difficult plays and the most immediate effect of McWhinnie's appointment was the import of a large number of foreign plays. Many of these plays had never been performed in British theatres and so it came about that, for a period of about ten years, the BBC Third Programme became the principal agency for the performance of plays which had previously been neglected in Britain. Though some of the plays of Anouilh had reached the British stage, others by Betti, Brecht, Buchner, Camus, Cocteau, Ghelderode, Puecher, Robles and Supervielle had their British debuts on radio. The effect of these plays upon young British writers was to break down some of the insularity which had for so long been a feature of the British theatre. But the task of translating and of adapting these foreign plays for radio also had cultural importance because they had to be brought away from their stage conventions.

But whether, for example, someone like McWhinnie was argu-

ing the case for the translation of a foreign play or for the performance of a play by a British writer, he was primarily driven by
his appreciation of the nature of the dramatic experience in radio.
In his *The Art Of Radio,* his first preoccupation is the nature of the
silence which surrounds the words. To some readers this interest
may appear fanciful and touched with some mysticism but, it had
very practical inspiration. The nature of ordinary speech had at
last been photographed very precisely by the tape-recorder. Like
the Impressionist painters whose eyes had been trained to know
the true nature of light, the writers had become aware of the
nature of silence. They were thus to become verbal technicians
and they were to become almost dictatorial in their determination
to have their lines spoken at the exact pace which the reality of the
tape-recorder had demonstrated. They were to be aided and
abetted by McWhinnie, Bray and Bakewell, who had also heard
the news from the tape-recorder. It should not be thought,
though, that this awareness of silence was achieved consciously.
It was simply a time when the writers and the radio producers
started listening in a different way. The failure to appreciate the
importance of this moment has led to some wild explanations of
motive and intention which have very little to do with what
actually happened when the nature of silence was revealed.

9.
The Drama School

An important factor in the development of drama in Britain in the fifties was the very close relationship which existed between the writers and the radio drama producers. Many writers, including Harold Pinter, Stan Barstow, Andrew Salkey, Alan Prior, Alan Ayckbourne, William Trevor and Jonathan Raban, have acknowledged the help and encouragement they received while working in close harmony with a radio producer. This close relationship between producer and the writer, who might be a novice to radio, is somewhat similar to that of an army sergeant teaching a recruit how to aim and fire on a rifle-range. The producer would know that he had discovered a potential marksman but he would then have to train the writer to focus his message correctly. In his *The Art Of Radio*, which he wrote after he left the BBC, McWhinnie has summarised some of the definitions and requirements which he so often had to impart to the writers. During an era when it was the general ambition to represent ordinary speech naturalistically, it is interesting that he was careful to define the limits which the writer must respect. He cites the speech in *On The Waterfront* as an example of a kind which on radio is not permissible. It is, he felt, at times too inaudible to convey reality and meaning. 'But radio cannot go this far,' he wrote. 'We cannot afford chaos or lack of intelligibility.' The audience cannot be left wondering what is going on. The naturalistic representation of ordinary speech needs to be fashioned and placed in a coherent setting. The pursuit of the new realism actually required a considerable artifice and the use of subtle sound effects and devices. Though the object might be to create a kind of play which did not sound at all like the accepted formality of the theatre, this creation required just as much craft and ingenuity. McWhinnie wrote:

Radio cannot aim at realism but only at the most persuasive illusion of reality; since every sound that comes out of the loudspeaker is significant the radio producer needs to look always for the most typical and evocative detail in order to build his sound picture; otherwise the ear is distracted and the image blurred. What is more, he must look for sounds which have not lost their immediacy through excessive use.

Tape-recorded effects and radiophonics were put to good use by McWhinnie and others in extending the vocabulary of sound effects. But there were by this time many sounds, like doors shutting, horses's hooves, and seagulls, which had become clichés and stock jokes in comedy shows like *The Goon Show*. It is relevant that an actor like John Gielgud also felt that too much noise could often impair a performance.

Speech and silence are the two most powerful factors of the living theatre. Their basic values have been distorted in this mechanical age by the new inventions — the gramaphone, transistor set, television, by amplification both in the theatre and the cinema. People live with a perpetual background of noise and it seems that many welcome such an accompaniment to prevent themselves feeling lonely and dissatisfied with the monotony of their daily occupations.[1]

He concludes therefore that the problem of projecting a subtle play in a large theatre is more challenging than it used to be. His problem as an actor dealing with an audience which has become accustomed to background noise is not quite the same as the one facing the radio playwright or producer. But people like McWhinnie learned quickly that the kind of embellishment which had worked brilliantly in the radio feature simply could not be used in the kind of radio play which now interested them. The grand manner employed to present Edward Sackville-West's *The Rescue* was totally wrong. McWhinnie, like so many of the playwrights whose work he admired and championed, also recognised the importance of silence.

The final ingredient in the creation of the radio illusion is silence. There is a not unnatural fallacy abroad that the air is there to be filled; a pause is a lapse is a chunk of dead air is a defeat; words and sounds must bombard the air without cease.[2]

And later, he wrote: 'There is one simple and vital fact governing radio form. The radio act comes out of silence, vibrates in the void and in the mind and returns to silence, like music.'

As an example of the way in which pace can affect the mood of a play, he cites Ugo Betti's *The Burnt Flower Bed*, which was translated by Henry Reed. He points out that the opening dialogue between Tomasco and Giovanni can sound quite happy if it is performed quickly but that their relationship changes when pauses are inserted.

It is not surprising that when such plays were read by those who were accustomed to another dramatic style, they were found wanting and mystifying. Bakewell has recalled the difficulties which he and McWhinnie faced in championing the plays of Beckett, Pinter and many others. According to him, the Third Programme was at that time committed to the traditional virtues of the radio feature and to broadcasts of the classics but was not particularly interested in original radio plays. Val Gielgud was devoted to a kind of drama which was important and noble and worthy. Bakewell says that his god was Ibsen and that his view was that plays should contain a high seriousness which was not easily apparent in this new drama. Bakewell's first trial of strength occurred when he cómmissioned Pinter to write *A Slight Ache*. The playwright had already had theatrical success with *The Birthday Party* and, in a manner which was to become very common in British radio, he and Bakewell simply talked over his ideas for the play until Bakewell was satisfied. But when the play was written, neither the Third Programme nor Gielgud could, according to Bakewell, see any point in it. Eventually they relented and the play was produced and hailed as a great success. It might be thought that this would have made acceptance of any subsequent play by Pinter slightly easier but Bakewell says that on every occasion the merits of subsequent plays had to be argued all over again. After McWhinnie had finally managed to broadcast Beckett's *All That Fall*, he had to argue the case for *Embers*, which Gielgud wanted to reject. In the case of Rhys Adrian's *Betsie*, Bakewell faced total opposition and he then

pleaded to be allowed to make a specimen production, employing Drama Repertory Company actors and using studios in slack
periods in the evenings. When he presented this production, the
Third Programme liked it and approved its broadcast. Something
similar later happened to the plays of Barry Bermange and it
would seem that the principal difficulty lay in appreciating the
true nature of these new plays when they were simply read on
the page and not heard.

It was not easy to appreciate what Rudiger Imhof, deliberately
giving the word a fresh meaning, has called the 'radioactivity' of
Pinter's plays. He remarks that *A Slight Ache* is 'radioactive' not
only because it exploits the potential ambiguity of silence in the
character of the mute match-seller, but also because it dramatises
the mental processes of the characters. He also points out that
when this play is performed on the stage or on television, a good
deal of its dramatic force is lost.

> The unresolved ambiguity of the silent match-seller is
> destroyed. The audience is confronted with a shabby old man,
> who is dressed in a shaggy fur-coat and lingers awkwardly on
> the stage. There can be no doubt then that the match-seller
> exists. His silent behaviour merely suggests that he is an idiot
> or, at best, a deaf-mute. Edward's and Flora's persistent
> attempts to elicit an answer from him become embarrassing.
> Edward is no longer competing with a figment of his imagina-
> tion but with a real person. The more concretely the match-
> seller is presented for the audience to either accept or reject, the
> more he loses his dramatic substance.[3]

Imhof adds that a further crucial element in the development of
the play on radio, the way in which the match-seller is presented
as growing younger while Edward grows older, simply cannot
be achieved on the stage or TV. It is perhaps understandable that
those who were trained to consider drama only as something
which could occur in a theatre and which might then suffer some
kind of adaptation in radio could not appreciate the subtleties
which were contained in plays of this kind. But the trials which
attended Bakewell's championship of *A Slight Ache* were as
nothing compared to the extraordinary saga attending the
passage of Beckett's play from Paris to British radio. The story

begins in March 1953, when Cecilia Reeves, the BBC's Paris representative, went to see *En Attendant Godot* in the company of Reyner Heppenstall. They thought it might be suited to the Third Programme and wrote to McWhinnie, enclosing a script. 'The first part of it is extraordinarily effective on the stage but it ceased to be convincing after we had a drink at the interval so that it would probably be easier to hold the attention with a radio version.'[4]

The script was then sent to E. J. King-Bull for his comments, which were as follows:

It is pretty funny. Performed visually by a troupe of genius it might be supremely funny. It is something of a Ted Kavanagh script in style, with suggestions of a Rene Clair production, as well as the more intellectual passages of Lewis Carroll. On top of this, there is presumably a philosophic or even religious allegory, which is sure to make some people mention Kafka.[5]

It was at first thought that the BBC should hire a translator but mercifully Beckett obliged with his own version in English. It was at this stage that Gielgud began to have second thoughts. He wrote in October 1953: 'I am left with the impression of something that is basically "phoney", and I was incidentally interested to see the notice in *The Times* last week on a production of the play in Germany which strongly confirmed this impression.'[6] Gielgud's feelings about the play were decisive and it was rejected and the script sent back to Cecilia Reeves in Paris in May 1955. Raymond Raikes then went to see the play performed at the Criterion Theatre, London, and began to argue its merits and in July 1956 John Morris, the Controller of the Third Programme, went to Paris to have lunch with Beckett. The playwright was at this time working on *All That Fall* and McWhinnie went over to Paris in the company of Patrick Magee, the actor, to discuss its production. Beckett later wrote to Morris that he had been very glad to meet McWhinnie. 'His ideas about the sound agreed with mine and I am sure he will do a very good job,' he wrote. The end result of this was that *All That Fall* was broadcast on 13 January 1956, nearly three years after Cecilia Reeves had first suggested that the BBC ought to take the Irish playwright seriously.

It would be easy to scoff at this curious reception of Beckett's work or to laugh at King-Bull's commentary, which compared *Waiting For Godot* to a script written by Ted Kavanagh for a comedy series. But those who have now turned Beckett's play into a very weary critical industry which devotes most of its effort towards the identification of hidden philosophy within the text should heed the reaction of one of the first people to read the play. King-Bull found it very funny, as indeed did the first theatre audiences in the days before the critics had persuaded theatre-goers to become intellectually self-conscious about Beckett's plays. It is sad that the earnest search for hidden meanings in a play like *Waiting For Godot* now imposes upon audiences a condition of reverent awe which prevents many people appreciating the jokes and the wit of the word-play which Beckett indulges in. It has to be said again that with Beckett, as with many other Irish writers like Joyce and Flann O'Brien, the first interest is in the use of language and in joy of exploiting its ambiguities. It is relevant that, as far as Beckett was concerned, the most important treasure which he and McWhinnie had in common was an agreement about the use of sound. They were not worrying about meanings; they were more interested in the technical setting for the words.

There was a way in which, at this time, one thing tended to lead to another. The close relationship between writers and radio producers meant that sometimes a writer would recommend the work of another. When *All That Fall* had been broadcast, for example, Beckett wrote to congratulate McWhinnie on the production and then added, almost as a postscript, that he had just seen a play by Marguerite Duras, called *Le Square*, which he commended. The result of this recommendation was to lead to yet another saga of rejection and eventual acceptance by the BBC. Reeves in Paris sent a copy of the play to Bray in London, remarking that though the play had been a flop on the stage in Paris, it might well be better suited to radio. Bray sent the play to Helena Wood and this is her report on it, dated 26 October 1956.

> This is distinguished, sensitive, poetic and intelligent, but it is also a little repetitive, too self-conscious and not a little pretentious. And it is not drama. Nothing happens, nobody does anything and only the bud of a situation is there. I think it would lose nearly all its quality on the air and become a crashing bore, unless we can cut drastically enough to eliminate

faults and reveal the piece for the excellent radio material it could be by virtue of its light but firm construction, atmosphere, evocative talk and sad penetration.[7]

This very excellent report is interesting because while Wood acknowledges the poetic quality and the evocative talk, she yet echoes the kind of view about drama which Bakewell has described as being the one held by Gielgud and others. She says that Le Square is not drama because nobody does anything and nothing happens. She was probably right to say that the play needed some cuts but she was clearly unable at that time to appreciate the nature of this kind of drama in which nothing appeared to be happening in the way in which theatrical tradition demanded. It is perhaps not surprising that despite Beckett's commendation the play was rejected but in 1957 Bray tried again and the play was finally broadcast, leading to a commission of Duras's Moderato Cantabile.

Ionesco's arrival in Britain was also somewhat chequered. Sasha Moorsom, who was a features producer, had been sent a copy of The Bald Prima Donna, which she passed to Bakewell, who was unable to get the play accepted. Bray therefore resorted to the device of commissioning Ionesco to write a play especially for radio. It was at the same time that Ionesco had been asked by Jean-Louis Barrault to write a play for the stage and the playwright then offered the same play, Rhinoceros, to both the French theatre and the BBC. It proved to be a greater success on radio than it was in the theatre and there is no doubt that its British radio performance considerably assisted in getting Ionesco's work known and appreciated in the British theatre. Something similar occurred to Arthur Adamov, whose political views made his work unacceptable on French radio and who owes his British reputation entirely to the broadcasting of his plays on radio.

The story of the struggle to broadcast plays by French playwrights during this period is only a part of the larger story of the way in which radio at this time became what Andrew Salkey once described as 'the first taker'. Young writers began to look first to the radio market rather than to the stage. The manner of working together on a script which the feature producers and writers had employed now spread to the drama studios. There was at last a congenial mood towards attempting new forms.

McWhinnie expressed this open-minded attitude very well in his book.

> If the old forms do not fit, the writer may invent new ones. He may be satisfied with conventional theatrical 'form', i.e. fairly substantial scenes confined within a limited space; he may even find the three-act form suitable for what he wishes to express, rather as Robert Bolt did in *The Last Of The Wine*; he may need the flexibility of film, an intricate pattern of short scenes, each with its own vividness but meaningless except in relation to the whole; an interior monologue, with or without the heightening of other sounds and voices, may serve his needs; he may wish to create an evocation of mood or atmosphere with no dramatic development of any kind; he may simply wish to tell a story.[8]

It seems to have been the case that many writers who are better known for their work in other forms have found radio's opportunity for story-telling very attractive. Ted Allan, who has written stage and television plays and scripted films, began his writing career in Montreal as a journalist. But he wrote what could be called the first drafts of all his later work in the form of radio plays. James Hanley wrote *Say Nothing* as a radio play. He then adapted it as a television play and then rewrote the story for a novel. William Trevor first wrote *Going Home* for radio. But when he was asked to adapt it to television, he found that he had first to rewrite in the short story form and he then adapted the short story to television. Trevor, who feels that there is something very boney about radio, regards it as a form which demands many of the disciplines required in the short story. The kind of rambling and self-indulgent narrative which may be condoned in a novel has no place in the short story, in which characters and their situations have to be defined immediately and with economy. Something of the same requirement is very necessary in radio, where the listener must be given immediate clues and hints as to character and place and time.

It is not perhaps surprising that this open-minded approach to the dramatic exploitation of radio prompted an interest in the merits of the dramatised short story and in the creation of interior monologues. It is significant that Bakewell, whose original interest was theatrical and directed towards the importation of foreign plays, had his own attitude changed by the radio experience. When he was not seeking out new plays, he turned towards the dramatised monologue. He arranged productions, for example, of Kafka's *Metamorphosis*, Joyce's *The Dead* and passages from Strindberg's *Inferno*, while McWhinnie produced Beckett's monologues. It might seem that such projects were merely exercises in having the works read aloud but they served to examine in close detail the problems of production and presentation of narrative. The actors did not merely read the texts; they performed them and responded to the heightening sound effects and they explored the dramatic factors lurking within works which had been intended for silent reading on the page. The original interest in coming as close as possible to the realities of ordinary speech gave way here to the need to acquire a new kind of formality. The style of performance nodded in the direction of ordinary speech but it also contained something of the tension of legend which is present in the manner of the traditional story-teller or *shannachie.* The listener was made conscious of the thinking within the words.

The view that, if the old forms did not fit, the writer might invent new ones naturally stimulated a tremendous response from writers who no longer felt that they were obliged to write in some defined or accepted form. In the late fifties and sixties, British writers tended to offer their ideas first to radio rather than to the theatre or the television studios. New writers all thought in radio terms and those who had earlier suffered rebuffs offered their works again. John Mortimer, who started his career writing scripts for the Crown Film Unit and who had in 1941 proposed a play presuming that Oscar Wilde was still alive at ninety and had had it rejected, now found a market for the adaptation of his novels.

His play *The Dock Brief* was first performed on radio in 1957 and reached the stage a year later. In the same year he also wrote *I Spy* for radio which reached the stage in 1959. The British radio studios became at this time the equivalent of the experimental and fringe theatres which developed in the seventies. But it had the important advantage of being staffed and managed by people whose criteria were professional rather than amateur and who still had to keep an eye on audience reactions. Though the writers were encouraged to try out new dramatic forms and methods, their work had to meet certain agreed standards of competence. Those who had previously written for the theatre not only enjoyed meeting this demand for competent and intelligent work; they enjoyed the manner of collaboration between actors, producers and studio technicians which was peculiar to the radio drama studio. Bernard Kops, for example, who had had some theatrical success with his *Hamlet Of Stepney Green*, had been distracted by the attendant publicity and welcomed the privacy which radio afforded and the opportunity it offered him to concentrate on what he was trying to say. Like many other writers he found that he could work better away from the limelight of publicity attending the theatre and could derive inspiration from the close-knit team of actors and technicians in the radio studio.[9]

Not all of the writers at this time who were later to write plays or novels or become film directors necessarily wrote plays. For example, John Boorman, the film director, started his career in radio and was for some time the chairman of a Youth Programme about the Arts. He served as a critic but he also did a number of radio talks and interviews and, significantly, compiled a series in which he interviewed film technicians on aspects of their work. Boorman was a member of the generation which had been brought up on radio and he feels that it exercised a great influence on his imagination and suggested freer dramatic forms and an immediacy which he feels is curiously more related to the film than to the theatre play.[10]

Another group of writers whose talents were later to find very various outlets and who began in much the same way as Boorman was the West Indian writers. Many of them, like Andrew Salkey, had been contributors to the BBC's Caribbean Service when they lived in the West Indies and radio had for many of them been their first publisher. When they arrived in London in the late fifties they naturally turned first to the Caribbean Service and continued contributing talks and short stories to it. But it was not long before writers like Jan Carew, Edgar Mittelholzer and George Lamming, together with Salkey, began to write feature programmes which they then found had a market not only in the Caribbean Service but also in the British Home Service. Salkey believes that this radio experience was very important and that it taught him the need for economy of expression and showed him the dangers of self-indulgent narrative.

It might be thought that such lessons could well be learned by the writer in private and without the aid of others, but there was at this time a particular atmosphere in the British radio studio which was peculiarly encouraging. There was, for example, a new approach on the part of drama producers which emulated the pattern of work once practised by feature producers in the era before the arrival of the portable tape-recorder. Although there was still the system whereby new writers submitted their plays to the Script department, where they were read and considered for production in a rather detached fashion, drama producers began to develop very close relationships with the writers in the manner in which Pinter and Bakewell got together to discuss *A Slight Ache* when it was still little more than an idea in the writer's head. Following such discussions, producers would then argue the case for a play to be commissioned and while a very few writers would sometimes insist that what was eventually broadcast was entirely the fruit of their own work and imaginings, it was often the case that the drama producers had played a significant part in the shaping of the plays.

In this workshop atmosphere the principal objective was to get the best out of the script and to get the play well done and there was a spirit in radio which set pride aside.

A good example of this kind of collaboration occurred when Tom Stoppard was working on his play *Albert's Bridge*. Stoppard is now thought of solely as a theatre playwright but his radio origins are very relevant to any study of his work. Like Boorman, he belonged to a generation whose dramatic education had largely been acquired by listening to the radio. He was an avid listener but it was not until he heard James Saunders's *Alas Poor Fred* that he was fired with the ambition to write something similar. It was at about this time that the BBC had instigated a series of new plays called *Just Before Midnight*, which were only of fifteen minutes duration. Stoppard felt that he could write for this series without necessarily committing himself to a lifelong career as a dramatist. He therefore wrote *The Dissolution Of Dominic Booth* and *M Is For Moon Among Other Things*. He also attempted a play about a husband who is trying to get through on the telephone to his wife, who is the Speaking Clock lady. All these plays were early essays in Stoppard's interest in the comedy of speech manners and they led him to write *Albert's Bridge*, which is about a man painting a bridge only to have to start painting it all over again the moment he has finished. Richard Imison received the play and invited Stoppard to come in and talk about it. Imison was unhappy about the ending, which he felt was inconclusive, and when they met and talked they hit upon the idea of ending it with a troop of soldiers marching across the bridge and failing to break step so that the bridge collapses. Stoppard then rewrote the ending to conclude with this collapse.

This kind of close collaboration, in which radio drama producers sometimes acted as textual editors and even assisted with the improvement of the plot, was standard practice at this time. Writers like Stoppard and Pinter and others tended to work with particular producers like David Thomson, R. D. Smith, Robin Midgley, John Gibson, John Tydeman and, of course, Michael Bakewell and Donald McWhinnie. Often these relationships developed from the original haphazard allocation of a producer to a particular play. When the writer submitted another play he tended to contact the producer who had done his first work.

Given this close working relationship, which naturally facilitated better standards, it is not surprising that many writers made good use of radio at this time. But this informal and friendly atmosphere was to be found only in London until the appointment of Alfred Bradley to the drama studios in Leeds in 1961. Bradley's part in encouraging several writers of distinction in the north of England has been exceptional. When he arrived in Leeds, northern writers who thought of writing for radio generally sent their scripts to London and there was therefore not a single play waiting for Bradley on his desk. He therefore began his task as a begetter of plays by travelling around to all the known writers in the area, inviting them to call in on him at any time. While the Leeds studios became an open house, Bradley also set up a programme called *Northern Drift*, which broadcast short stories and talks and poems. Like the BBC's Caribbean Service, which had given West Indians a beginning, *Northern Drift* attracted new writers who, having written a short story, would then be encouraged by Bradley to try their hand at a play. The list of those who would readily admit some debt to him includes Stan Barstow, Henry Livings, Don Haworth, John Arden, Alan Plater and Allan Prior. Alan Ayckbourne, who started his career as a radio drama producer, also owes some inspiration to the Bradley treatment.

It should not be thought, though, that because all these writers had connections with the Leeds studios, they belonged to any definable school or movement associated with the north. Bradley encouraged them but he did not attempt to mould their work in any way. He adopted the McWhinnie principle that all or any form should be attempted if that was the writer's particular desire. Barstow's association with Bradley assisted the writing of later novels, while Allan Prior was to become a very proficient script-writer for television series like Z Cars.

Naturally the approach of all these writers tended to have a northern emphasis but, while Ayckbourne was to find his métier in stage comedy, Arden was to strive towards a more serious statement which yet contained elements of dialect speech in a heightened and poetic form.

There was a feeling at this time that writers could try almost anything and that the radio drama producers would aid and abet them. David Rudkin, for instance, began with translations. He had just given up working as a teacher and, wanting to keep up his knowledge of Greek, wrote to Imison suggesting that he translate a play of Aeschylus. He originally had Seven Against Thebes in mind but ended up translating The Persians. And from this venture in translation was eventually to come his play Afore Night Come. This was not a time when it was presumed that a writer must always write a play like the last one. It can be argued that there were social and historical forces at work at this time which were demanding a new kind of drama and a fresh dramatic mirror to current events. But though this was a time of change, when Britain was divesting herself of Empire and there was a regeneration of intellectual and artistic interest in the provinces, it is doubtful whether the dramatic explosion which occurred at this time would have been possible without the assistance of radio. Even though Gielgud admitted that he was baffled by many of the plays, and some would say that he was often excessively hostile to this new work, he deserves some recognition for his part in making sure that drama, whether he liked all of it or not, was allowed to thrive on British radio. At a time when television had become the mass entertainer and radio was only serving a minority audience, it was he who argued the case for sustaining the output of plays which was many times the capacity of all the theatres in Britain. In the course of time, many of the plays which were first heard on radio were transferred to the stage and many of the writers who first wrote plays for radio later found outlets in the theatre and television. It is a mistake to assume that the sudden flowering of British drama in the sixties had any other origin except that of the radio studio but it must also be said that this flowering had much to do with producers like McWhinnie, Bakewell and Bradley, who acted as catalysts and who, on occasion, had to resort to subterfuges in order to get the plays heard.

10.
The Radio Shape

Some part of the confusion attending the critical reception of some of the plays which came to the theatre via radio is due to a failure to appreciate their origins and to take sufficient account of what Bakewell calls their 'radio shape'. While Cooper's plays were acclaimed by the small group of radio drama critics, they were often greeted with some bemusement in the theatre. They have a radio shape and they also employ devices which, when watched in a theatre, invite conclusions which were not intended. Radio's ability to employ a kind of dramatic shorthand which may move the listener swiftly from one apparent state to another age or to the inner recesses of the minds of the speakers cannot be easily represented in the theatre. What Raban has called the privilege of not needing to worry about the actors' appearance or their exact moves on the stage invites the use of very swift scene changes and moods. What may be implied or hinted at in a radio play has to be spelled out on the stage and, if it is not so spelled out, the critics looking for deeper meanings tend to seize upon these hints and develop extraordinary theories.

The action in Cooper's plays moves very easily from apparent portraits of reality, decorated with closely observed imitations of ordinary dialogue and its customary clichés, into and out of fantasies which are touched with delicate satire. Even among the radio people, arguments used to break out as to whether his plays were too avant-garde for the Home Service or too straightforward for the Third Programme. It should have been more clear but too often people still wanted to know what he was really saying; it is something of an irony that, of all his contemporaries, Cooper was actually saying something quite definite about the society which surrounded him. Many of his heroes are people who are trapped in the machinery of contemporary life and who are unable to escape. At a time when most critics were looking for plays with a heavy political message or some essay in post-anarchist confusion, this comparatively simple message, which had considerable relevance, was often disregarded.

In her paper at the Durham Conference, Frances Gray provided a very concise definition of the Cooper hero. 'He finds the modern world too much for him; he stands on a chaos composed of political complication, corrupt authority, trashy consumer goods and stifling bureaucracy; he writhes like an insect on a pin, baffled and impotent.'[1] This kind of hero was not, of course, special to Cooper. Other radio playwrights sometimes featured the same kind of character in situations similar to those which Cooper chose. Rhys Adrian in his play *The Bridge* depicts a suburban married couple on a picnic trip into the countryside. They reiterate the commonplaces of speech which are the sad by-products of their trivial round and common task. The husband is glad to find a picnic spot in unspoiled country but he then encounters a countryman who is glad that this beauty spot will soon be destroyed by a motorway. He looks forward to not having to work on a Sunday and being able to go on picnics. MacNeice also employed a Cooper hero in Roger Malandine, who is a sports commentator in *One Eye Wild*. Malandine's marriage is on the rocks and when his wife leaves him in the middle of a cricket commentary he crosses a road carelessly and is run over. In his concussed state, he dreams a series of high adventures in which he is a knight in armour engaged in a tournament, is a hero of the First World War and is killed heroically in the Second World War. Malandine is yet another example of the Cooper hero, who is so often a man for whom there are no heroic causes left and who must suffer the trivia of the supermarket society.

In *Under The Loofah Tree*, for example, Cooper employs a contrivance similar to the use of a concussed state in MacNeice's *One Eye Wild*. Edward Thwaite is dreaming in a hot bath of moments of imagined grandeur in which he recalls his old headmaster, his army sergeant, a radio quiz-master and his parents. He imagines himself winning the Victoria Cross and taking part bravely in a radio quiz, but he also tries to drown himself. At the end, though, he simply gets out of his bath and returns to his normal banal condition.

In this world of trivia, where large heroes are out of place, the Cooper hero sometimes yearns for the place in the historical spotlight but sometimes becomes obsessed by the meaningless chaos and clobber of the consumer society. In *Before The Monday*, a girl delivering flowers encounters a man who wishes to die because he has become overwhelmed by the astronomical complexities of life. He cannot shave, for example, because this act reminds him of the mining of iron ore and its complex conversion into stainless steel blades. He cannot eat sardines because this would force him to consider the ramifications of the tin coming from Peruvian mines and of the Portugese fishing for the sardines. The packaged world appals him but the girl asks him to take life as it comes and to accept things as they are. She eventually persuades him to forsake his obsession but Cooper does not resolve the matter there. While the hero goes off happily to church, having ceased worrying about shaving and eating sardines, the girl hears the church bells and begins, as the play ends, to think about the complexities of bell-ringing.

This sardonic touch is also to be found in *A Crown Of Gold*, where the central figure is again a social misfit who does not, however, engage in the customary asides and inner doubts. He is Max, a steward on a yacht owned by Sir Ronald and Lady Pinn who are descended from most of the royal families of Europe. Though he is a refugee he does not take well to his menial work and Sir Ronald solves his problem by taking him to an island off the coast of South America. Sir Ronald virtually owns this island, which is currently having a revolution. The revolutionaries threaten to shoot Sir Ronald but he outwits them by giving them Max as their constitutional monarch. This satire on the possible continuing usefulness of constitutional monarchy contains less of the usual soliloquy to be found in Cooper's plays and it could perhaps be converted into a film, but it still contains a subtlety which makes it peculiarly attractive on radio.

This subtlety, which allows such swift changes of scene and of mood within mood and which may be assisted in English by the use of dialects and speech styles which immediately tell the British listener what kind of person is speaking, does not always transfer easily to the stage. But in spite of this, there have been some stage plays which employ this kind of delicacy. Armand

Salacrou's stage play *The Unknown Woman Of Arras,* which was translated by Robert Baldick and adapted to radio by Frederick Bradnum, has many of the Cooper radio elements. It opens with a classic theatrical occasion when the hero, Ulysses, discovers that his wife Yolande has been unfaithful and so shoots himself. There then follows a play which really should have been written for radio. The body of the dying man takes part in a series of scenes with people from his past life. He meets his grandfather, who died in battle at the age of twenty. His best friend appears at the ages of twenty and thirty-seven. All the women in Ulysses' life are brought forward to taunt him for his cruelty, his forgetfulness and his insincerity. Among them is a woman he once met during the First World War at Arras and his relationship with her is presented as the only true one because it never came to a conclusion.

Such a play can certainly be staged but is obviously more suited to radio in the way that MacNeice's *One Eye Wild* is. The presentation of the friend of Ulysses at different ages is, for example, difficult on the stage. When a character indulges in a reverie and calls up the memory of old friends from his past, he may summon them on the radio with almost the same speed as a solitary person thinking himself of past events. On the stage, these people have to appear and move before they can speak; their presence imposes a break upon the flow of thought which is the speciality of the radio plays of MacNeice and Cooper. Stage presentation of some of Cooper's plays has tended to emphasise their comic aspects and to obscure the tragedy so often contained within the wry satire.

The radio shape of Cooper's *Mathry Beacon* or of MacNeice's last play *Persons From Porlock* is such that it defies simple adaptation to the theatre. *Persons From Porlock* is the biography of a painter who is both haunted by and deflected from his beckoning muse. He is tempted by commercialism and waylaid by artistic vogues. He is a drinker and veers from one woman to another but, in the end, the muse speaks clearly to him and he returns to his true forte and paints huge caves which are like cathedrals. In a sense the play is autobiographical in that MacNeice also had to fight off various influences which deflected him from his vocation as a poet, but it is also an important commentary on the place of the artist or writer in an age when the

world offered many chances for persons from Porlock to inter-
rupt their work. There is no statement here which could be made
across the footlights and what is said is not contained within the
formula of a play of debate. As with all good radio plays, the
mental action moves too fast, evoking images which would not
have the same chance of being enjoyed in a theatre.

The fact that two of the best British radio playwrights did not
easily translate into the theatre does not mean that their work had
no influence. The many playwrights who started in radio also
listened to the examples of Cooper and MacNeice, who showed
how a play could now be set in any time or place and how the
action could be moved on the hinge, perhaps, of a single word.
They should not be given all the credit but their examples may
well have inspired some of those who began to write a kind of
history play, which was not the costume drama of the West End
theatre and was not couched in the fustian speech which had
previously been associated with such plays. The revolution in
diction went beyond the need to represent ordinary speech as it
really was and persuaded some writers that historical figures
might speak this language too. Robert Bolt's *The Drunken Sailor*,
set on a British corvette in 1800, is an example of this style and the
radio shape of it was to influence his later style in the theatre.
Bakewell even argues that it was Bolt's radio shape which inspired Whiting when he came to write *The Devils*.

The new kind of history play could also use its setting to
discuss matters which were of more contemporary importance,
as in the case of Alun Owen's *The Rough And Ready Lot* and John
Arden's *Sergeant Musgrave's Dance*.

Owen's play is set in the 1870s in a South American republic
but the debate it contains is reminiscent of the debate which had
attended the bombing of the monastery at Monte Cassino in Italy
in 1944. The mercenary officers of a revolutionary army are confronted with a monastery which has been turned into a strong-
point. Captain Morgan, a Welshman who has advanced beyond
Nonconformism to the point where God is dead, believes the
monastery must be destroyed. He is faced with Captain O'Keefe,
a devout Irish Catholic, who is only interested in the victory of
true religion. But there is also Captain Kelly, an Irish pragmatist
who has no sympathy with either of these devout extremes. Their
Colonel, a Yorkshireman, has no interest in the moral issues and

would avoid them if he could. O'Keefe brings the moral argument to a conclusion by spiking Captain Morgan's guns but Morgan finds a trophy cannon and when O'Keefe tries to stop him firing it, it explodes and kills them both. The explosion is heard by the defenders of the monastery, who then desert their stronghold, fearing an attack. The way is then open for victory but the Colonel's Indian camp follower, who reveres the site because the monastery is built upon an Indian shrine, thinks that he has ordered an attack upon it and she therefore kills him. The only man left is Kelly, the man with no pride and a wish simply to live and get by.

Owen manages to summarise the states of mind of the religious bigots but he also presents an interesting study of the English character in the Colonel. As long as the Colonel can avoid moral issues he leaves them alone. He is kind because self-interest requires him to be so. His view of life is that it is ruled by the practical needs of the immediate moment. It should be no surprise that this play, which was first done on radio, had some considerable success in the theatre. But, like Arden's *Sergeant Musgrave's Dance*, it had a radio shape.

Arden's play also employed an historical allegory without making its point too bluntly. It was possible to reflect that, though it was set in a northern mining town in the nineteenth century, it invited some parallels with the presence at that time of the British Army in Cyprus. The mining town is cut off by snow and the miners are on strike. The Mayor and the Parson, the custodians of law and order, welcome the arrival of Sergeant Musgrave and four soldiers, who they imagine have come to quell the strike. But Musgrave and his men have only come to the town to bring back the skeleton of one of their comrades who has died in a colonial war abroad. Arden's theme is the complicity of everybody in any action which is taken in their name and he fully exposes the hypocrisy of the Mayor and the Parson, but this play is also something of a landmark in its use of language. It does not merely employ Yorkshire dialect to give the lines a kind of naturalism. It employs dialect syntax and phrases in such a way as to give them a heightened meaning and a kind of poetry of the ordinary remark. The Yorkshire speech is placed in a new context which gives the ordinary phrase greater significance and meaning. It is sometimes assumed that Brecht alone is the main influence upon Arden's work but this is to neglect Brecht's own indebtedness to radio which he shared with Arden.

Another work which owes a great deal to its radio origins and which also tackled an event in the remote past was Ingmar Bergman's film *The Seventh Seal*, which the Swedish film director first wrote as a radio play called *Tremölning — A Painting On Wood*. This play was inspired by the murals which are a common feature of churches in central and southern Sweden and they must have been familiar to Bergman from his early childhood because his father was a pastor. *A Painting On Wood* is a much simpler work than *The Seventh Seal* and recalls a similar essay by Peter Gurney, called *The Foundling*, in which voices are given to the gargoyles and carvings in East Anglian churches. When Bergman converted the radio original to film he had to invent a coherent narrative and to provide the figures with some form of interaction which is not present in *A Painting On Wood*. This necessary adaptation evoked some enthusiastic critical interpretations of the film, which was thought to be suggesting, among other things, a parallel between the Black Death and the H-bomb. But when the original radio play is studied and heard, it is apparent that Bergman's objective was much more innocent and straightforward and that he started out simply to give voices to the painted figures in Swedish churches.

The opportunity to tell history afresh was especially inviting in radio because the writer could present his or her characters without having to present them in costume and without period settings. There was also the temptation to tell again some of the stories which had become encrusted with heroic legend. Three samples of this kind of work are H. A. L. Craig's *The Flight Of The Earls*, Francis Dillon's *The World Encompassed* and MacNeice's *They Met On Good Friday*. All these plays owed something of their structure and approach to the style originally pioneered by the Features department. They presented their figures and events in a perspective which acknowledged that the old stories were being told afresh. Craig's play dealt with the departure from Ireland of The O'Neill and The O'Donnell and he made the sharp contemporary comment running contrary to the received legend, that their flight was inevitable. They were accompanied by their harpers and Craig reminded the listener that their reputation and legend owed much to those who had sung their praises. But there was no attempt here to have the chieftains speak lines of grandiose fustian and their dilemma was argued in modern colloquialisms which gave the subject much greater point. The same approach to the diction was made by Dillon, who recounted Drake's circumnavigation of the world. Drake spoke as a Devon man, which he was, and was no longer heard intoning like some patrician monument. And whereas earlier celebrations of this voyage might have dealt only with the grand moments, Dillon spared several scenes to the dispute which broke out during the voyage between Drake and Doughty.

The emphasis placed upon this dispute, which earlier cele-brants of this national maritime hero tended to ignore, may be compared to the fresh historical perspective which MacNeice applied to the circumstances leading up to the Battle of Clontarf in 1014, when the Vikings assembled to meet the army of the Irish King just north of Dublin. The story which MacNeice had to tell was much more complicated and was much less well known than the one which Dillon told afresh. MacNeice's narrative sometimes suggested the manner of a sports commentator or a war correspondent, and this was necessary. Like Dillon, MacNeice did not dress up the speech of the various historical figures in archaic language and he thus brought home to the listener something of the real nature of the event.

Radio can naturally treat history in this way just as it may deal with current affairs. The actors are not to be seen dressed in costume, which, in the theatre and on television and in film, seems sometimes to provoke the demand, even on the part of the actors, that the language should be similarly attired in antique verbiage. Despite the fact that Shakespeare did not employ such language in his history plays and merely used the heightened and poetic version of contemporary speech, there is a mistaken tradition that olden days must be presented in an olden diction. It is interesting that it seems never to have occurred to a writer like Rosemary Anne Sisson, who has written a number of history plays for television, including *The Six Wives Of Henry VIII*, to employ this antique diction. Her model was not, in fact, a radio play but George Daviot's theatre play *Richard of Bordeaux*, which was singularly free of this archaic speech. When she wrote her first play *The Queen And The Welshman* for theatre and subsequently adapted it for radio, she wrote the play in contemporary English, and though Daviot's play was her model there can be no doubt that she was also influenced by the rendering of history in radio, which had already established this different form of presenting the language of historical figures.

The opportunity to present history plays where only the voice mattered and the costly scenery and costumes was of no account also appealed to some writers, like Bolt and Arden, because they also offered the chance to present the play of debate. At a time when it was the vogue to present close facsimiles of Wordsworth's low and rustic speech, there was the consequence of a limitation on the types of character who could be heard representing this kind of speech. Excepting the satirical studies of writers like Cooper, it was not the custom to write plays in which the contemporary captains and the kings took part. When a play was set in a dosshouse the characters might credibly be heard discussing death and decay and human folly but they could not realistically discuss matters of state. They could, of course, mutter about the evils of, for example, capitalism or state control but they were not in the position socially where their opinions could have any real relevance. Writers who wished therefore to write plays of debate which examined some of the contemporary political and social issues sometimes took the remedy of writing historical plays. A play which depicted a debate involving the captains and the kings of the past could present situations and dilemmas which had contemporary analogies. British radio naturally aided this development because the fashion had long been established of presenting historical documentaries and also because it embraced the policy of broadcasting plays from abroad and from the past which were often historical plays anyway. But the new historical drama also employed the style of diction commonly found in other contemporary plays so that, for example, Drake was at last heard to be a Devon man and not some patrician figure on a linguistic pedestal. The use of contemporary speech styles in history plays also emphasised the connection between the issues being raised and discussed and similar contemporary issues. But it has to be said that this particular radio development has not yet made its influence wholly felt in the theatre, where there is still a prejudice in some quarters in favour of plays in which the characters are expected to utter phrases like 'By my halidom' and 'Egad'. Some part of this prejudice has been eroded in television, where the presentation of history largely in close-up renders this archaic language rather absurd and where the radio example has been fairly closely followed.

Not all the history chosen in plays at this time was from the remote past. Saunders Lewis, for example, chose to write in Welsh his play called *Treason* which dealt with the bomb plot against Hitler in 1944. This play, which was broadcast in 1959, studied the states of mind prevailing among members of the German command in France as they waited for the telephone call from Berlin to tell them whether their treason had prospered and if Hitler were dead. But the legend that the Officer Corps could have saved Europe is exposed when von Kluge, the key man in France, is shown to be captive to the Third Reich because of a monetary debt to his leader. The military aristocrats who first encouraged the dictator are shown to be the victims of their own folly. Lewis argues that, for all their professed altruism, the leaders of the bomb plot were still in love with the idea of fighting again another day under a more respectable leader. The play, which was translated by Elwyn Jones, was performed by a wholly Welsh cast which allowed the merits of the play to be seen in their true perspective. The play is not, after all, a piece of propaganda; it is an examination of the motives and dilemmas of the traitor.

It was in the same year (1959) that British listeners were at last given a chance to hear another of Tyrone Guthrie's plays which demonstrated that the theatrical director had not lost his radio touch. Guthrie's *Mitchenor's Dog* had a shape which was significantly very similar to some of the plays now being regarded as avant-garde. Like so many of the plays at this time, it was in the form of a monologue. An elderly nurse is speaking her thoughts aloud as she tends an old army officer who has been paralysed by a stroke. In the distance a dog barks and the nurse remarks upon the cruelty of those who stone a tethered animal; an observation which refers obliquely to the condition of her patient. She chatters to herself about her relationship to the world beyond the sick-bed but within the radio context this reference, which is supported by sound effects, is more convincing that it would be in the theatre. Guthrie was here making the kind of point which he had first made more than thirty years earlier and it was fitting that this play should be broadcast during the second period of discovery and innovation in British radio.

Guthrie, who was one of the pioneers of radio drama, confirmed in this play the view of many younger writers that one of the most suitable radio forms was that in which the main character is engaged in some very localised activity which can be easily defined by sound effects and verbal cues and which can then be the credible basis for an extended monologue. When this form has been transferred to the theatre some critical confusion has necessarily arisen. The extended monologue written for radio tends to raise questions in the theatre which it never sought to answer. Persons engaged in conveying streams of consciousness are not always advantaged by being seen upon a stage. Their dress and appearance and the stage settings may inadvertently offer additional messages which were not originally intended by the author. That which has been written only to be heard may not always carry the same message when the work is also seen. It was this realisation which caused so many writers who had written for radio to become very particular about stage directions and movements.

The success of writers like MacNeice and Cooper and Guthrie in exploiting the confines of the radio shape may seem to some to resemble a dramatic exercise comparable to standing on only one leg. The exceptionally good radio play cannot be satisfactorily transferred to the stage without some loss of its intensity and without some unpremeditated additions to its original meaning and context. But this is not to say that this work had no influence on theatre drama. It demonstrated the need for a much more closely observed diction and it also pointed towards the need for a style of speech which would take account of the fact that while a character is speaking he or she may be thinking about something else. Supplementing the ideas of Stanislavsky and the consequent pursuit of Method acting, the writers gained more practical experience in radio where it was realised that it was not enough simply to present the words and that the actors should be encouraged to present characters with a past which existed before the action of the play commenced.

It is strange, but little critical attention was paid at the time to the way in which the plays of MacNeice and Cooper often presented this previous history. In *Persons From Porlock*, MacNeice sets out, of course, to present a deliberate biography but, for some reason, Cooper's heroes were presumed merely to be slightly comic and not possessing much serious social comment. But it needs to be said that his portraits of lost and baffled middle-class conformists in an age of prosperous consumer capitalism were more accurate than many of the politically committed studies which were offered during the same period. It is probably for this reason that they were often misunderstood; Cooper's social observation was too sharp. It was presumed that because they offered such close studies of the clichés of ordinary conversation they were only essays in the comedy of speech manners. It is odd, but few would have presumed that Dillon's presentation of Drake as a Devon man was merely such an exercise and most would recognise the greater value given to his historical study by paying such close attention to speech manners. The emphasis placed upon economy in speech and upon giving historical characters more than a place on a pedestal also encouraged a new approach to the history play and to a new style of production of such plays in the theatre where Guthrie, needless to say, had been one of the pioneers of a new approach to production. The siting of the action in any place or time by the means of very calculated and minimal effects and of verbal cues of the kind practised with mastery by Cooper and MacNeice also freed dramatists from the kind of set which their predecessors had accepted. This freedom of choice of dramatic location prepared some writers, like Bolt, for the writing of films. It might be asked why Cooper did not convert his plays into films and the answer is that though they offered examples to others, they were too good as radio plays to suffer such conversion.

Their form was so specifically designed for radio performance that they did not transfer well into performance in the theatre. For those who may only have the opportunity of reading Cooper's plays in script form, it is hard to convey their special radio quality. To appreciate them fully they have to be heard. The fact that they had this special quality does not, however, mean that they had no influence on theatre drama, for it has to be remembered that other writers also listened to Cooper's plays with great attention during a period when the radio in Britain offered the most extensive repertoire of both British and foreign plays. His plays were a seminal influence on the work of many British dramatists.

11.
Technical Advances

The fact that some of the dramatic forms which radio has encouraged cannot be transferred easily to stage or screen can be used to argue that radio writing is a peripheral literary and dramatic activity. It was this view which was adopted by some British literary critics who believed that a poet like MacNeice was wasting his time in radio when he ought to have been devoting himself to his proper task as a poet. It is certainly true that since MacNeice's death and the development of techniques like stereophony and binaural sound there has been a development towards a dramatic form which can only work within radio, but it should not be thought that even this work has had no influence upon dramatic writing for the stage. The language which radio demanded and inspired has had considerable influence upon contemporary dramatic diction and has argued in consequence some changes in dramatic structure. Some of the dramatic forms which radio invited had had no counterpart in the theatre, but their development, even though it often had no theatrical application, was to have its important influences.

In his preface to *The Rescue*, Sackville-West draws attention to the fact that dramatic factors are involved in some forms of radio performance which do not come into the category of straight drama.

> Radio is in fact susceptible of carrying far more *degrees* of dramatisation than the stage or screen because of the extreme flexibility of the medium and its wide powers of imaginative suggestion. Even the straight 'talk' has an element of drama in it, conferred by the listener's focus on the personality of the unseen speaker, and by the shape of the talk itself, which has to be designed to grip and hold attention from first to last.

Listeners to regular broadcasters like Alistair Cooke, who has broadcast a weekly *Letter From America* for a number of years, would recognise immediately the dramatic factor involved and the speaker's capacity to grip and hold the attention while he unravels his theme. Cooke's brief is ostensibly to report as a journalist on current affairs in the USA but in the course of time he has established such a rapport with his listeners that he may approach almost any subject in a tangential fashion. Gripping the attention with seemingly irrelevant anecdotage, he will then move with surprising speed into some very clear-sighted analyses of American life and politics. Though his task is that of the journalist, he is actually involved in a form of dramatised story-telling and though he may give the impression that he is merely speaking his thoughts aloud in a casual and off-hand manner, his weekly talks are structured to hold and grip the attention and they provide a good example of the kind of talk which Sackville-West had in mind. Another broadcaster who practised this method well was Cutforth, who began with war reports and who later applied the same kind of anecdotal quality to his documentaries. If we set aside for a moment the embellishments of the feature documentary when it is accompanied by special music and effects, we may note that this form is essentially that of a radio talk which is then illustrated by inserts, which in the early days were read by actors and were later replaced by actuality tape-recordings. In such a radio feature the writer– presenter offers a specific thesis which is then decorated and illumined by the inserts but when they are composed and narrated by someone who conveys a presence, a dramatic quality is conveyed to the listener.

The radio style of giving the impression that the narrator is only thinking aloud naturally lends itself to the presentation of other voices illustrating the theme. But it was also a form which was to lead to the creation of a form of radio play which is peculiarly suited to the medium and which generally defies transference to the stage. It was not dramatically difficult to convey to the listener that the central character was thinking aloud and recalling the voices of others associated with past events in the manner employed by the radio reporter. This form may sometimes present a kind of autobiography or an aural form of the novel but it has the attraction of economies which cannot be achieved on the printed page as when, for example, the characters by their voices and accents convey within a few moments their likely social position and previous history.

This aural form of the novel was one which occurred to Guthrie as early as 1928 when he wrote *The Flowers Are Not For You To Pick.* The listener is given the swift cue at the opening that Edward, a failed clergyman of Anglo-Irish stock, is drowning in the South China Sea and is recalling his past life and his family. MacNeice frequently employed this same device and made brilliant use of it in 1944 when he wrote *He Had A Date,* a play which is a kind of obituary for his friend, Lieutenant Graham Shepard, who died on an Atlantic convoy during the Second World War. Reggie Smith, who regards this as one of MacNeice's finest works, has said that the poet felt that it had failed but he feels that this sense of failure was due to his very personal involvement. Smith likens the play to a private newsreel of Shepard's life. In his final speech, Shepard is heard to say: 'And I leave nothing behind me – child, work or deed to remember. But I tried, you know. I tried. Believe it or not, I did have ideals of a sort. But I could not quite get the bearing. Now let me sleep; I'm tired.'

This speech appears to address the listener directly but the presentation is such as to make it appear that these thoughts are only being overheard. And once the convention is established that the audience is listening to the thoughts of a drowning man, it is of course easy to switch very swiftly to the speech of friends and others who are remembered by the central figure. Such assemblies of voices from past or present cannot be adapted with any success on the stage and it is, in any case, of the essence of this dramatic form that the central figure must only be heard. An adaptation which, for example, employed the Brechtian device of a narrator who points out such a figure to the audience would destroy the essential privacy of thought which MacNeice conveys. The listener is brought much closer to the dilemmas and regrets and joys of the narrating character than could ever be achieved on the stage. His biography, which stretches from childhood to the arrested moment of his death, at which the action takes place, touches in a passing way on a kind of parable which is ambiguous.

He is not presenting a thesis to be demonstrated by the supporting characters. Some part of the drama is taking place within the narrating character. It might be possible to adapt this radio form to film, in which the voice of a character like Shepherd would be heard in 'voice over' narration but, though this technique might overcome some of the difficulties, it would be a poor substitute for the radio experience. The action in a film cannot move with the pace which radio can achieve and the necessary swift changes of scene would baffle a cinema audience. The story could, of course, be presented in book form but it would lose the qualities of presence contributed by the actors and it would need the kind of total rewriting which William Trevor had to resort to when he sought to convert a radio play to television.

In his *Persons From Porlock*, MacNeice was to make use again of this particular radio form when he presented the fictional biography of an artist of his time. His purpose in such works is to convey the broad canvas of the life and times of his central characters, recording their crises and their moments of triumph and disillusionment. Such works generally treated the whole of a life rather than some particular moment of crisis. It was left to other writers to create yet another radio form, which could be described as the aural short story. While MacNeice utilised the device of the interior monologue within his radio plays, other writers made the interior monologue the basis of their works. In such plays, the listener is never expected to stray far in imagination from the immediate surroundings of the central character, who usually tells his story as if he is being overheard by accident or, like the good radio reporters, is merely thinking aloud. This form seems to have found great appeal in Germany and Hermann Kesser's *Nurse Henrietta*, which was broadcast in translation in Britain in 1959, provides a good example of this genre. The play, which lasts an hour, eavesdrops on Henrietta on the morning of her appearance in court to give evidence on the death of a doctor she has loved. She could have prevented his suicide but did not do so because she feared that when he recovered from his illness he would return to his wife. A man has been accused of his death and Henrietta is torn between the need to protect herself and her respect for justice.

Another German play which reached British radio at this time was Dieter Wellershoff's *The Minotaur* which involved two monologues. A man is waiting while his girl-friend goes off to have an abortion. He is full of guilt for forcing her to do so but his conflict of emotion is not resolved when she comes back to tell him that her doctor is not available. The play ends with their relationship breaking up. Like *Nurse Henrietta*, this play places the characters under a microscopic focus of attention in which every intake of breath is heavy with meaning. Something of the same intensity of focus was present in James Hanley's *Gobbet*, which was not conceived in quite the same manner as a monologue piece but which had something of the same force. Hanley presents a ventriloquist who employs his dwarf son as a dummy. After a grotesque scene in a hospital he knows that he must kill his son and while the secret that the son is not a dummy is kept from the stage audience, the listener is made aware of the truth in a private conversation between father and son. When the father finally kills his son on stage, half the audience roars with laughter because they think the figure on stage is only a dummy while the rest scream with horror because they know the truth. The device which is employed here, a character who is presented both as dummy and as living, could not be employed on the stage or in film with the same success and though the work is structured to display other voices it hangs entirely upon the voice of the father in the style of interior monologue.

Hanley's plays, which often placed the listener in the position of overhearing a confession which gripped and held attention, usually moved out from the closed monologue into a traditional dramatic structure involving dialogue between the central figure and others. But his model was unfortunately not the one which found most favour. In Germany, in particular, a style of radio play was developed which served more limited and almost wholly literary rather than dramatic intentions. This was to lead to a rather self-conscious approach which emphasised the fact that the listener was in fact only listening to a radio, and ushered in the device of having, for example, a writer writing about being a writer.

Friedrich Dürrenmatt won an Italia Prize in 1958 with a play of this kind called *One Evening In Late Autumn*. Its convoluted plot involved a famous writer of crime stories who is confronted by a man who maintains that he is in fact the actual murderer of all the victims in his stories. This man is forced to fall from a window and the play ends with the writer dictating again his radio play. The sincere attempt made here to acknowledge alienation and to expose the mechanics of plot and of literary artifice may be commendable but its example was to lead to the creation of some rather self-conscious creations which featured writers writing about writing and which became no more than literary conundrums.

This development coincided with the acquisition of sound techniques like stereophony and binaural sound which at first seemed to promise greater flexibility in radio drama production. The solitary figure in the confessional location could now be even more perfectly represented in a naturalistic manner. But it was quickly found that the representation of exterior effects was made harder rather than easier. In 1958, for example, Cleverdon found that when he sought to make a stereophonic production of Carroll's *Alice In Wonderland*, and wanted to depict Alice bathing in her tears, the splashing of water in the studio was not satisfactory and he had to go to the trouble of taking his actress to a swimming-bath to gain the correct effect. The ingenious creation of effects which had sufficed in monaural productions to provide an image for the listener was no longer practical. To create exterior locations naturalistically it was necessary to adopt the sound techniques practised in the making of actuality film for television or cinema newsreel. As this was not always feasible, there was a tendency to restrict the use of stereophonic production to the type of play which featured the interior monologue capable of being controlled within the studio. This was to lead also to a new approach to radio drama production which tended to destroy the group relationship between actors, the writer, the technicians and the producer which had been artistically very fruitful.

These technical improvements now allowed the producer to record actors in isolation, to assemble the necessary sound effects and to weld these various components together in the privacy of an editing room. Such a method could be more efficient than the previous system but it could also create the kind of production which no longer had the same tension and sense of presence that had characterised radio plays when they were put together by the group of actors and technicians working together. Another problem created by stereophonic sound was the seeming advantage it provided of at last being able to differentiate movements to either left or right. In monaural productions, it had always been the practice to indicate such movement by moving towards or away from the microphone, leaving the listener to determine the possible leftward or rightward direction taken by the character. Stereo now invited this left or right movement to be spelled out and it was at first thought that this capacity would enhance the radio production of stage plays. But like the need for Alice to be recorded in a swimming-pool, it was a device which actually got in the way and it was to be some years before producers like John Tydeman overcame this technical bounty by dispensing with its offer to create right and left movement and by regarding stereo's shape as a globe rather than as a stage. In this way, the stereophonic effect is merely used to give depth to a form of production which is still conceived in monaural terms. But in the early days of stereophony the emphasis upon making the technique work preoccupied the producers and sometimes came between the good relationship they had once enjoyed with the writers, who had generally looked upon radio as a dramatic arena in which they were freed from the constraints demanded in the theatre. This technical improvement did not therefore immediately stimulate fresh dramatic endeavour on the part of the writers and to some extent it actually inhibited them. Though they had enjoyed the meticulous determination of pace and the representation of natural speech, they were less ready to respond to the new requirements of stereophonic production.

Most writers for radio in Britain tended to continue to write in monaural terms, leaving stereophonic adjustment to the producers. They could argue that the added sense of reality provided by stereophonic production was still dependent upon choice of words and upon a convincing plot and story. Realistic presentation of natural conditions by means of stereophony can achieve little if the dialogue is not convincing and the listener is not gripped to know what is going to happen next. Radio drama thrives upon this need to compel the audience's attention in a manner which caused Marshall McLuhan to describe radio as a hot medium as opposed to television, which he called a cool medium. It is arguable that his observation was based on styles of television production which were then current and which paid less attention than they ought to have done to the verbal content at the expense of conveying a satisfactory visual message. But in attempting this rather arbitrary distinction, McLuhan confirms from the listener's point of view the degree to which radio is capable of generating a greater tension. This capacity is wholly under the control of the writer who must know that he needs, in Sackville-West's words, to grip and hold the attention from first to last.

This necessary focus of attention on the way of telling the story, whether it be for a radio talk or a play, was to inform the approach of many writers who later wrote novels and who began by writing monologue plays for radio. In Germany this particular form came to be regarded as the only dramatic form peculiar to radio, while in Britain it remained only one of the forms, providing the basis for plays like Hanley's *Gobbet*, which moves towards a more formal dramatic structure and contains the kind of interaction which is not possible in the aural short-story form of the interior monologue. There was in any case a preference in favour of the traditional dramatic forms which was encouraged by Gielgud and by Martin Esslin, who succeeded him as head of Radio Drama in 1963. On the part of the writers there was also an attitude which regarded the radio as a form of experimental theatre in which it was possible to try out ideas which might later find acceptance on the stage.

While writers like N. F. Simpson and Pinter continued offering their work to radio while enjoying theatrical success, younger writers like Joe Orton and Colin Finbow submitted their first plays to radio. Their ambition was mainly theatrical and they had no wish to write purely for radio. But the medium offered them an opportunity the theatre could not always provide. Though they could not count upon much critical attention in newspapers and magazines, which have rarely paid radio the attention it has deserved in Britain, they could know that their work would be performed by actors of national reputation and that they could draw upon the expertise and advice of drama producers whose knowledge of drama in general was far greater than that of a director of a fringe of experimental theatre. It is relevant, for example, that the shaping of much of Orton's early work owes much to the assistance which John Tydeman gave him. This shaping did not, however, lead the writer towards creating work specifically designed only for radio. The emphasis in BBC radio drama was less upon the creation of radio forms like the interior monologue than upon exploiting the dramatic qualities of plot and characterisation which are not necessarily wholly dependent upon radio's techniques. This is not to say, though, that there were no experiments employing the new technology. Some of the producers who had started in features, like Bridson and Nesta Pain, who had been responsible for engaging the talents of people like John Mortimer, William Golding and Alan Sillitoe, tried out stereophonic effects. The establishment in 1958 of the Radiophonic Workshop, which was to spawn a whole generation of sound technicians who later moved into films and television, led immediately to works like Frederick Bradnum's *Private Dreams and Public Nightmares* and J. M. Weston's *The Princess Royal*, both of which explored new ways of relating words, sound and music. These experiments generally followed the established tradition in British radio features of creating a kind of opera of the spoken word in which the sound effects were still the servant of the word.

In Britain, the French vogue for the pure abstractions of *musique concret* had less appeal. The invitation to create almost any kind of sound which had no obvious relationship to the traditional forms of music inspired by the dance, or to a form of mumbling not related to any recognisable linguistic form, was not readily accepted. The pure abstraction was largely thought impractical and a more favoured approach was that of *Words And Music*, in which Beckett provided the verbal side of a diaogue between himself and his cousin John Beckett, who supplied the musical responses. The poet George MacBeth, who was then a Talks producer, also exploited the new techniques in his radiophonic settings of *Sono-Montage* by Rosemary Tonks and of *ABC In Sound* by Bob Cobbings. Another significant effort at this time was William Russo's stereophonic jazz opera *The Island*, for which Adrian Mitchell supplied the libretto. But it could not be really said that any of these works represented an attempt at the creation of an abstract form. The new sounds of radiophonics and the dimensions of stereophony were generally employed to embellish a coherent and intelligible piece of verbal communication in much the same way as the earlier features producers had used specially written music to heighten and flavour their scripts.

There were several social factors peculiar to British radio which made the pursuit of some kind of abstract radio form unlikely.

There was, for a start, the very close cultural interaction between the radio studios and the theatre in London. Despite some of the misunderstandings which have already been described, radio drama in Britain had always had a bias towards the theatre. Broadcasting House was not, in any case, ever an isolated radio station inhabited by people who were isolated from other cultural activities and who were thus persuaded to pursue some abstract and purely radio form. And even when producers have wanted their writers to try and break new ground, they have sometimes found this very difficult. Bradley, who has tried very hard to persuade his northern writers to try out new ideas, thinks that one of the causes of failure is the influence upon the writers' thinking of the enormous output of radio plays by the BBC. The young writer with fresh and extravagant ideas is bound to have been influenced consciously and unconsciously by listening to the 200 to 300 plays which are broadcast each year. This output has created a standard consensus which the new writer imitates to some extent, whether he or she wishes to or not. There is therefore an acceptance of the established forms which renders it more difficult to break into new ones.

But the relative failure of British radio playwrights to develop beyond the pioneer work of writers like Guthrie, MacNeice and Cooper and of producers like Bridson, Cleverdon and Dillon, to say nothing of the work of McWhinnie, has to be balanced against the fact that the BBC has provided British writers with an extraordinary stimulus which has subsequently altered literary and dramatic approaches in other fields. Even though the pursuit of pure radio form has been rather neglected, the medium in Britain has forced almost everyone who has written for it to pay much closer attention to narrative structure, to the immediate creation of character and to the need for a fierce economy of dialogue. This need has been as much felt by dramatists as by those who have contributed talks or news reports. Rene Cutforth once said that the broadcaster must write his script as if he is broadcasting and then speak his script as if he is not. What he is recognising here is the way in which the speaker must overcome the barrier between himself and the listener without resorting to the alienating device of announcing that he is engaging in an artificial form of communication. Cutforth and Cooke, and Cooke's predecessor Raymond Gramm Swing, all practise the art of conveying their personal presence first and of then presenting their subject in a tangential manner, as if they have only just thought about it. They overcome the potential creation of alienation by presuming that it does not exist and such broadcasters do not ever attempt to give their audiences a formal lecture.

A similar approach seems to have inspired most dramatists in Britain who have used the radio. Whether their plays have been set in the remote past or in distant parts, they have been primarily concerned to create immediately this sense of presence in the listeners' minds.

For many of them, the additional facility of stereophony has seemed paradoxically to be something of an impediment. Jonathan Raban, yet another writer who has used radio as a workshop, expressed this reservation well when he referred to what he called stereophony's high infidelity.

> To a small handful of plays, stereophony adds a quality of dense, subtly textured realism which is unavailable in a mono production. Stereo is an excellent tool for fleshing out certain atmospheric ideas; it can bring the illusion of all the sounds of a particular event into the listener's own room. Some plays are enhanced by it but, for many, stereo is a straitjacket. It tends to impose a mechanical naturalism on everything it records. It keeps sounds 'out there', making it hard to create that special, intimate 'in here' quality which was once the hall-mark of radio drama.

He illustrates this by comparing a stereophonic production of Thomas's *Under Milk Wood* to the original mono production. Remarking that several critics found that the play suffered a curious diminution of its power in this stereo production, he felt that when the play was placed in a 'real' (that is to say, stereophonic) Welsh village, its language sounded arch and stilted. The transmission of what the poet had intended to be received as a dream taking place within the minds of the listener was prevented. Raban's reservations would have found support among many of those who wrote for radio when mono production was the only means of production available. They were not very interested in the creation of abstract forms of pure radio or in writing plays which acknowledged the fact that they were employing the mechanical and alienating device of the radio. They sought to go above all that, overcoming the audience's disbelief by presenting the convention that the legend or vision they conveyed was taking place in what Raban calls 'in here'. They spoke directly to the minds of their listeners.

12.
Conclusions

It is not advisable to study any form of creative activity without taking into account its social context and the practical conditions which to some considerable extent predetermine its method. This is especially true of drama, which must depend for success upon an immediate rapport with its audience. The audiences which attended the Greek classic theatre, the Elizabethan theatre, the French salon theatre of the eighteenth century, the Dublin theatre of Synge and O'Casey and the West End theatre of London in the thirties expected a dramatic style and manner of presentation suited to their particular tastes. The shape and dimensions of the arena, of the custom-built theatre or of the salon required different styles of presentation which demanded varying dramatic styles. The approach of the playwright to the creation of an entertainment to serve the occasion of a Miracle Play had obviously to be different from that which is involved in the writing of a play for the social intimacy of an élite group gathered in a salon in a royal palace.

It would be foolish to imagine that dramatists do not take such practical considerations of the *mise-en-scène* into account when they have written their plays. Unfortunately, the Romantic notion still lingers, suggesting that the creation of art is an end in itself and that its practitioners are demi-gods presuming the right to self-expression with scant regard for the opinions and tastes of the public at large. This notion persuades some that there is some ideal of pure art which must be fashioned by people who must not and do not take any account of market reactions. This leads to the assumption that those who serve the needs of a mass audience must inevitably demean their talents and it is likely that it is this assumption which has led to the general critical disregard of radio drama and to the failure to appreciate its influence and importance. It ought to be recognised that the dramatist, whatever his talents as poet or philosopher, must first be concerned with the practical matter of communicating his ideas to his audience and its particular condition.

It may be thought improper to suggest, for example, that Shakespeare, who was made relatively wealthy by his plays, paid some attention to the matter of getting his plays across to his audience. But Wolfit, who was a great collector of theatrical folklore, was fairly convinced that his favourite playwright took an intense interest in the commercial success of his plays. Apart from knowing that Burbage and Garrick entered stage left in Act III of *King Lear* and that Irving entered stage right, this great actor once explained to me the origin of the expression common to British actors: 'Has the Ghost walked?'. This query is a means of asking when they are to be paid and Wolfit maintained that it derived from the fact that Shakespeare usually played the Ghost in *Hamlet*. Until the Ghost had walked, the playwright could not go front of house to collect the takings. Even if this story is apocryphal and Shakespeare did not play the Ghost, the association of the Ghost walking and the actors being paid must surely relate to the occasion of *Hamlet,* which remains a great box-office success. This success is not merely due to the fact that it contains some sublime poetry; it contains a compelling story which has been put together by a craftsman who was an expert in the practical matter of theatrical communication.

In any dramatic form it follows that the writer's first consideration must be the selection of a manner of presentation which will best suit the physical conditions of the medium or arena or theatre in which it is to be performed. But when a new form or medium is established it naturally takes the writers some time and several mistakes before they find out how best to utilise it. When radio started it is not surprising that there was little attempt on the part of the writers or the radio drama producers to formulate theories in advance of practice. Their initial approach was generally rather haphazard and they spent a deal of time finding out what did not and could not work. It was soon obvious to them that the accepted style of performance in the theatre was unsuitable and that it would not be practicable to broadcast live theatrical performances. Because radio plays were usually broadcast only once there was no opportunity, as there is in the theatre, to alter and improve a production in the light of comments by informed members of the audience.

Though listeners were encouraged to voice their criticisms, it has to be remembered that they were also in the course of learning how to listen to radio and that those who had some knowledge and experience of drama were naturally trained on the theatrical model, which often had no relevance to radio. But apart from finding the right style of presentation, which was mainly the concern of the radio drama producers, the writers faced some other difficulties. The structure of the stage play, which may present a form of equation in which plot, character and situation are aided by visible movements and responses, is not suitable. The very first speeches in a radio play or radio adaptation of a stage play must provide the listener with instant clues as to the characters' social status, mental attitudes and previous history. Such clues can be imparted to some extent by the tone and manner of the actors' voices, but closely observed representations of accent and speech traits indicating the characters' social status and age are not in themselves enough. The writer must provide very accurate transcripts of speech styles which typify the characters. It is also necessary to provide during the opening scene some account or reference to preceding events which have bearing upon the action. Such accounts must not, however, be made too obviously. The method which Shakespeare employed in the second scene in *Henry V*, in which the Archbishop of Canterbury makes some long speeches providing a potted history of Anglo-French affairs, is not suited to radio. On the stage the audience is well aware that it is being provided with relevant background information but its presentation can be enjoyed because it is cloaked with some ceremony of movement and a sense of pageant in the telling. But the radio audience cannot see these princes moving and if the writer indulges in the same device as in *Henry V* the listener swiftly presumes that he lacks the skill to impart such information by implication and inference. On some occasions, radio playwrights have solved this particular dilemma by starting their plays with a short and simple statement provided by an announcer. Guthrie, for example, lets an announcer provide a swift clue at the start of his *The Flowers Are Not For You To Pick* when he observes that a drowning man is said to remember scenes from his past life. This short statement sets the scene and the convention of the play does not get in the way or seem to be too much of an intervention.

It was, of course, also recognised at an early date that radio could be used to tell a story overtly. In the absence of a large number of scripts specifically written for radio, it was soon the practice in British radio to present adaptations of classic novels. But those who adapted such works found themselves torn between adhering to the sequence of the novel's plot and attempting a fuller translation of the story to suit radio's requirements. The method of story-telling in a novel is often far too leisurely for radio. The writer may deliberately or even inadvertently fail to disclose some failing or hidden ambition on the part of a character but on radio the audience generally requires such information at the outset. Radio certainly encouraged a drama which narrated, but the form of this narration was subtly different to that which is often found in the novel. The narrative radio play which was to have its consequences in the theatre seemed to be one of the obvious ways of overcoming the problems created by an unseeing audience. In Brecht's epic theatre, the narrator becomes a deliberate artifice announcing the relationship between the audience and what is seen on the stage, in the manner of a lecturer in physics displaying equations on a blackboard. But while such a demonstrative manner may work quite well in the theatre it does not always succeed in radio. The listener is already very conscious of Brecht's alienation effect and the writer therefore has to create a subtler narrative form which implants characters and scenes within the mind's eye of the listener. It was soon found, for example, that the narrator could not easily adopt the manner of the presenter of a feature documentary programme, maintaining a distant tone of voice. The narrator in an adaptation of one of Hardy's novels had to suggest the bucolic quality associated with the people he describes. But here again, such characterisation of the narrator could sometimes go too far. A method of story-telling designed as a bridge between the dramatic action and the listener could of itself become a barrier.

Many writers who have written for radio have observed that it has taught them economy. It has helped them learn how many words to leave out and has made them appreciate the need for understatement. It is perhaps not surprising that so many poets have been attracted to it. It certainly seemed to offer them the kind of opportunity which Compton Mackenzie compared to that of Homer's relationship with his audience but they soon learned that their interest and skill in rhythms and language had peculiar application to the disciplines of the new medium. It is instructive that though Bridson chose to imitate the rhythms of Scott's poetry in his *March Of The '45*, neither he nor his fellow poets chose such a poetic diction again. It was soon clear that such a rhythmic style could impose upon the meaning and that its drum-beat distracts the listener. MacLeish and MacNeice learned early that they could not indulge in the sustained beat or in complex imagery. As a poet, MacNeice was very aware of the dangers of employing a formal verse pattern which, by trumpeting its presence, actually impedes communication. In programmes whose purpose was that of propaganda, a style of exhortation consciously exploiting a high rhetoric naturally has its uses but in a play the objective must be more devious. It is not surprising that MacNeice therefore came to favour the use of allegory and parable, which offers ideas in parallel rather than in the style of Brecht's epic theatre.

It must be stressed, though, that MacNeice and his contemporaries did not work out this manner of approach in accord with any preconceived theories relating to radio drama. He was never given to discussing theories of composition and was generally obsessed by the need for meticulous phrasing and linguistic precision. Such a preoccupation ought to be common to every writer in the English language, which with its huge vocabulary offers such a continuous embarrassment of verbal choice. But when one writes only to be heard and not read on a page or seen on a stage or screen, this preoccupation becomes a necessary obsession.

The supporting effects of music and sound effects may help to establish moods and particular environments but they can usually only succeed when they are cued by verbal hints and allusions. The hinge relating music and effects to the dialogue is verbal; it must be so written as not to appear too obvious and the words employed must be rational and cogent. It has been thought by those who aspired to the kind of abstract forms established in music and painting and sculpture that drama should also attempt such abstractions. But such abstract forms can have little place in drama, where the language must be coherent and rational if it is to communicate. The arrival of *musique concret* and the provision of new techniques like that of radiophonics seemed at first to suggest that radio could essay some kind of abstract form. But while the abstract attracted the interest of composers, it did not and could not appeal to writers who were tied to the word. In radio, where the spectacle in the mind has to be conjured into being wholly by the meticulous use of words, the idea of a play employing some abstract form of language was quickly seen to be absurd.

But apart from making the writers aware of the need to exercise rigid verbal discipline and to seek closer approximations to ordinary speech, radio also placed drama in a new social context. In countries like Britain, with a state monopoly system emanating from the capital, there was a demand for plays which would speak to all sections of the national society rather than to a select social group. In the twenties and thirties the need to entertain this national audience was used to argue a fairly strict censorship which tended to exclude the avant-garde for fear such work might cause offence. Even some of the plays of Ibsen had to wait the occasion of the outbreak of war before their merits could be argued and allowed on radio. But in the forties and fifties this negative and paternalistic attitude disappeared and the dramatists could suddenly write for the whole nation. It so happens that this opportunity coincided with a period of considerable social change which, like previous similar periods of change, tended to stimulate dramatic talent. During periods when societies have been relatively stable, the theatre has generally served socially exclusive audiences and its playwrights have provided witty and well-made plays which often contained caricatures of those the audience regards as social inferiors. But during periods of social mobility, like the fifties and sixties in Britain, the social composition of the audience tends to be less predictable and the dramatist is then exercised to present plays which will appeal to all and sundry without causing offence. It is worth recalling that the Elizabethan theatre also flowered during a period of considerable social movement and that it had to serve a random audience which not only contained the wealthy and the intelligent but had to speak to this social élite in the hearing of the groundlings. A somewhat similar condition was implicit in radio and the dramatist could no longer write for a socially select group. But during the twenties and thirties, the theatrical tradition was still very strong and it is something of an irony that the genesis of the dramatic revolution of the late fifties in Britain was almost entirely due to the work of people like Harding, Gilliam, Dillon and Bridson who pioneered feature documentaries. They realised that the credibility of the programmes depended upon the contribution of comments from people in all classes of society. Harding's dictum that the voices of the people must be heard may have had a political inspiration but it also served a practical need. The size and weight of early recording equipment made it difficult to obtain natural unrehearsed speech from contributors but the work of the feature producers opened up the forum to those whose voices were not considered cultured.

By the time the new wave of dramatists broke through in the late fifties, television had actually replaced radio as the mass medium but the fact that the radio audience was then in decline made little difference to the new playwrights. From their childhood they had looked upon radio as their only communicator and, in the absence at that time of fringe theatres and theatre groups, they looked first to radio as the natural market for their work. Unlike their predecessors, they had not been schooled in an esoteric theatrical tradition and because many of them were of provincial origin they found no difficulty in representing the natural manners of ordinary speech. The evidence provided by the portable tape-recorder, which revealed the silences and hesitations and *non sequiturs* of normal speech, merely served to confirm their personal experience and observation.

But there was more to it than this. There was a revival among English writers of that eloquence which Professor John Braidwood notes as being a characteristic of the Elizabethan theatre. 'The Elizabethans (or better, the Tudors) discovered that the hitherto despised vernacular could be used with magnificent rhetorical effect, could even, because it was a living language of greater flexibility and inventiveness, surpass the traditional Latin.'[1]

Braidwood goes on to regret that this natural eloquence of the Elizabethans was later stultified by the grammarians and that only the Irish writers preserved the gift of the gab. But in the late fifties and sixties, English writers who entered the theatres via the training ground of the radio studios turned again to the inspiration of the vernacular. Like Ben Jonson, whose father was a bricklayer, they were familiar with the strength of the vernacular, which had been hitherto despised, and they employed it to create a new eloquence. They also had the good fortune to be writing at a time when radio's enormous dramatic repertoire had widened the experience of their audiences and had brought together the rich in the balconies and the groundlings in the one theatre of the air. It is not surprising, either, that in this era the writers eschewed the kind of punctuation which the grammarians demanded on the printed page and that, like Elizabethans, they punctuated to indicate pauses of breath and the hesitations of ordinary speech. The kind of stage directions employed by theatrical playwrights in the thirties in Britain, which presumed that the pace of delivery and the manner of presentation should be wholly in the hands of the actors and producers, was no longer satisfactory. Radio had taught them the need to stipulate exactly the pace of dialogue and had made them aware that, for example, a scene intended to have tragic overtones could easily sound comic if the words were gabbled. Radio also focused attention on the need for economy and great care in the use of individual words. It made the actors listen too and it once caused Wolfit to complain that a playwright had used the word 'nothing' too early in a play. His Shakespearian experience had taught him that such a word should not be used carelessly and that it should be employed at the moment when its meaning had full purpose.

This intense interest in the exploitation of the vernacular was largely limited to Britain and nothing similar could or did occur in the USA, where there had never been the same cultural and social antipathy towards the use of demotic speech. American writers did not experience the same excitement of rediscovering the bones of language and those who started their careers in radio moved quite naturally into the scripting of cinema films in a manner which was not possible in Britain. The British film industry had never offered the writer a market comparable to that of Hollywood and those who started by writing plays for radio moved naturally towards the theatre. It is no accident that this period of flourishing drama in the fifties and sixties witnessed many contributions from Irish and Welsh writers who had always written for the ear and not the page, and that some of the new writers were the sons of *emigrés* who had spent their child-hood learning to be precise in the use of their adopted language. It has sometimes been supposed that many of these writers were primarily motivated by political and philosophical preoccupations but, while such motivations sometimes played a part, the most important influence on most of the work of this period was the rediscovery of the eloquence of the vernacular. It was learned again that the best rhetoric may sometimes whisper, that a sigh may well say more than a lengthy speech and that, above all, all speech grows out of silence.

The general critical failure to appreciate the contribution which radio has made to British drama is regrettable but under-standable. The fact that it served a mass audience led easily to the intellectual canard that it could not be of any cultural significance. The fact that while it could provide serials and series of little intellectual importance it could also give, through Rudkin's translation, *The Persians* of Aeschylus the largest single audience this play had ever known, was overlooked. The single broadcast of a radio play, followed by one solitary repeat performance, does not create the sense of social occasion to be found in the theatre and has not attracted the attention of many dramatic critics. The reception of a radio play by the listener is a very private occasion and does not stimulate the kind of debate which can attend a theatrical production.

Many of those who wrote for radio and who stimulated others to do so were not generally given to self-conscious regard for their work or to thoughtful analysis of their achievements. They were under continuous pressure to serve the immediate needs of what MacNeice referred to as 'the tall transmitters'. Remini-scences of this period of enormous inventiveness tend therefore to concentrate on anecdote and gossip rather than on a serious appreciation of what was achieved and McWhinnie's *The Art Of Radio* is almost the only reliable statement by one of these practi-tioners. The radio people have themselves done very little to answer the intellectual assumption that their work was of little cultural significance and the work of those who would now wish to review their contribution is not easy. Many of the early plays were broadcast live and were not recorded. Though the scripts are available, very few have been published in book form. Though some of the later plays have survived in recordings, a curious lack of entrepreneurial enterprise on the part of the BBC, whose officials plead the legal difficulties involved in publishing such productions, means that very few plays are available on cassette tapes. It may be thought by some critics that such recordings are not necessary to an understanding of the plays but they should be warned that any study of the scripts without being able to hear the recordings must necessarily lead to imperfect understanding. Though the meticulously annotated scripts of writers like MacNeice may appear to describe everything that happened in the studio, they cannot convey the magic which was present when the words, the music and the effects were woven together by the actors, the musicians and the sound technicians. The close association of writers and actors engendered in radio often meant that a writer stipulated a particular actor for a part whose aural presence imparted more to the presentation than can be gleaned from reading the script. It is, for example, one experience to read Beckett's *Krapp's Last Tape* and quite another to hear Patrick Magee performing it.

The fact that it is not enough to read a radio script in silence in order to appreciate it is a reminder that radio drama is a social as well as an artistic creation. In its heyday during the fifties and sixties it was the focus for many dramatists who, even when they later achieved success in the theatre, would return to radio to work out their next play. Since that period the opportunities for marketing a play have widened considerably and radio is no longer the obvious market for the beginner. It might be thought that the creation of Local Radio stations situated in provincial towns, where there are repertory theatres employing actors, could offer the beginner similar opportunities. But the emphasis in Local Radio is placed more upon creating disc-jockey programmes and public service programmes than upon dramatic production. The young writer in the eighties might well find the equivalent celebration of his fledgeling work in provincial television and might not any longer think first of radio, which, saving the Manchester studios, no longer emanates the passion and sense of immediacy which characterised the London studios in the sixties. But the fact that writers no longer feel that radio is the world's wonder and that the poets can no longer write narratives for radio features, which now depend upon the disciplines of tape-editing rather than on the construction of the emotive phrase, does not diminish its singular contribution. It celebrated the word and the breath that gave it life. It bred again a generation of writers who knew that they must listen while they wrote. It provided this workshop where there was no room for self-indulgent experiments and where the play had to speak to the various ears of a national audience. In Britain, of course, it can still do this.

Notes and References

2. The Conflict between Theatre and Radio

1. Val Gielgud, *Years in a Mirror* (Bodley Head, 1965).
2. W. M. S. Russell, Radio Literature Conference Papers (Durham, 1977) vol. 1, p. 12.

3. The Need for Narration

1. Julian MacLaren Ross file, BBC Written Archives, Caversham, Berks.
2. Michael Korda, *Charmed Lives* (London: Allen Lane, 1980).
3. Eckhard Breitinger, Radio Literature Conference Papers, vol. 1, p. 75.
4. Archibald McLeish, *The Fall of the City*, a radio play (1937).
5. Bertholt Brecht, 'Theatre for Learning', trans. Edith Anderson (Victoria, Australia: Meanjin, 1958) vol. xvii/3.
6. Ibid.

4. The Revolution in Diction

1. D. G. Bridson, *Prospero and Ariel* (Gollancz, 1971).
2. Ibid.
3. Ibid.
4. Tyrone Guthrie file, BBC Written Archives.
5. Ibid.
6. Personal communication to author.

5. The National Theatre

1. Louis MacNeice, Autumn Sequel (Faber).
2. Val Gielgud file, BBC Written Archives.
3. This unhappy event was witnessed by the author's uncle, the late F. C. G. Rodger, when serving in the same regiment.

4. Harman Grisewood, *One Thing At A Time* (Hutchinson, 1968).

5. Bridson, *Prospero and Ariel*, p. 76.

6. Barbara Coulton, *Louis MacNeice In The BBC* (Faber, 1980).

7. Personal remark to author.

8. Eric Linklater, *The Cornerstones* (Macmillan, 1944).

9. Eric Linklater file, BBC Written Archives.

10. Louis MacNeice, *Christopher Columbus*, a radio play (Faber, 1944).

11. Louis MacNeice file, BBC Written Archives.

12. MacNeice, *Christopher Columbus*, pp. 88–9.

13. Coulton, *Louis MacNeice In The BBC*, p. 67.

6. The Arrival of the Poets

1. MacNeice, *Autumn Sequel*.

2. Bridson, *Prospero and Ariel*, p. 179.

3. Ibid.

4. Bernard Kops, *Interview in a Secret Workshop*, BBC feature programme, 1977.

5. Coulton, *Louis MacNeice In The BBC*, p. 82.

6. Douglas Cleverdon, *The Art of Radio in Britain*, monograph for UNESCO (unpublished).

7. Donald McWhinnie, *The Art of Radio*, p. 67.

7. The Influence of Features

1. Peter Black, *The Biggest Aspidistra In The World* (BBC, 1972) pp. 173–4.

9. The Drama School

1. John Gielgud, *Stage Directions*, p. 14.

2. McWhinnie, *The Art of Radio*, p. 88.

3. Rudiger Imhof, Radio Literature Conference papers, vol. 2, p. 199.

4. Samuel Beckett file, BBC Written Archives.

5. Ibid.

6. Ibid.

7. Ibid.

8. McWhinnie, *The Art of Radio*, p. 95.

9. Kops, *Interview in a Secret Workshop*.

10. John Boorman, letter to author.

10. The Radio Shape

1. Frances Gray, Radio Literature Conference Papers, vol. 2, p. 175.

12. Conclusions

1. John Braidwood, *Ulster and Elizabethan English*, quoted by Benedict Kiely, *The English Language in Ireland*, Thomas Davis Lectures (Cork: Mercier Press/R.T.E., 1977).

Bibliography

ERIK BARNOUW, *A Tower In Babel,* a history of broadcasting in the
United States (New York, 1966–70).

PETER BLACK, *The Biggest Aspidistra In The World* (BBC, 1972).

D. G. BRIDSON, *Prospero and Ariel* (Gollancz, 1971).

DOUGLAS CLEVERDON, *The Art of Radio in Britain,* monograph for
UNESCO, unpublished.

BARBARA COULTON, *Louis MacNeice In The BBC* (Faber, 1980).

JOHN GIELGUD, *Stage Directions* (London, 1963).

VAL GIELGUD, *Years In A Mirror* (The Bodley Head, 1965).

HARMAN GRISEWOOD, *One Thing At A Time* (Hutchinson, 1968).

HORST PRIESNITZ, *Das Englische Hörspiel* (Dusseldorf: August
Bagel, 1977).

——————— *Das Englische 'radio play' seit 1945* (Berlin: Erich
Schmidt, 1978).

LANCELOT SIEVEKING, *Memoirs* (unpublished).

JOHN SNAGGE AND MICHAEL BARSLEY, *Those Vintage Years Of Radio*
(Pitman Publishing, 1972).

RADIO LITERATURE CONFERENCE papers, vols 1 and 11 (Department of English, Durham University, 1977).

Index